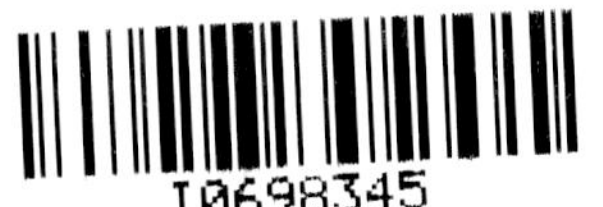

Prehistoric Palette: Coloring the Dinosaurs

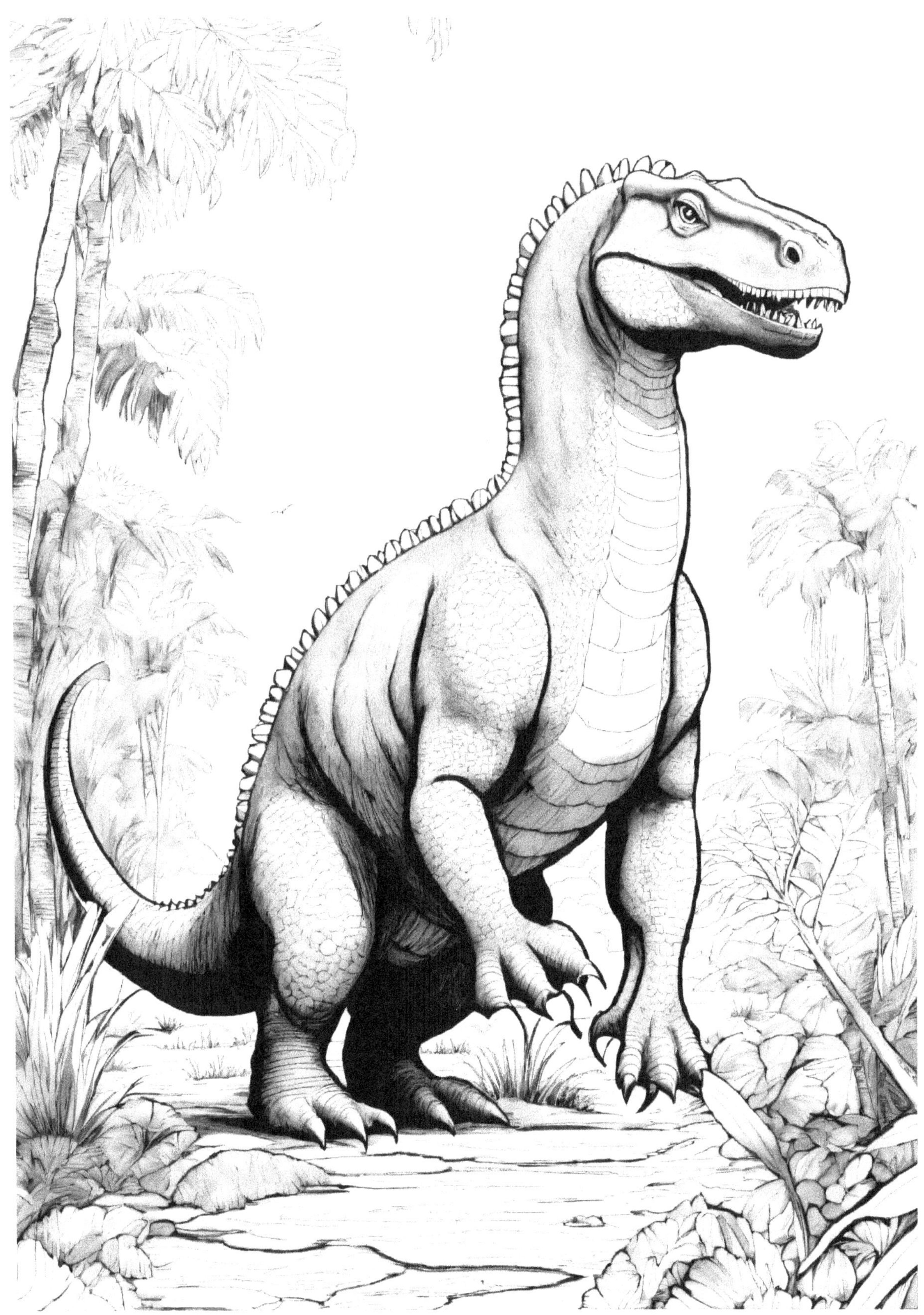

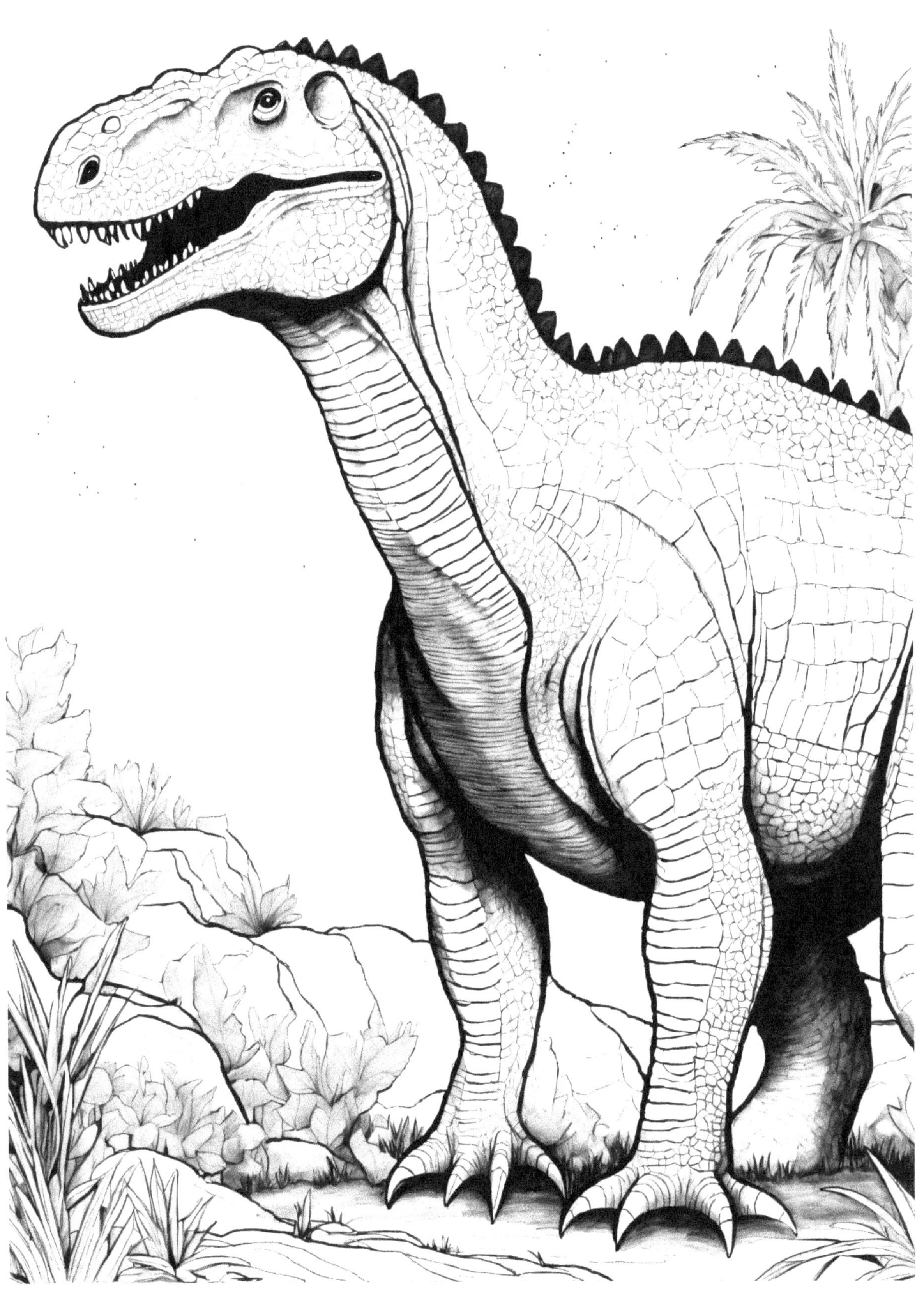

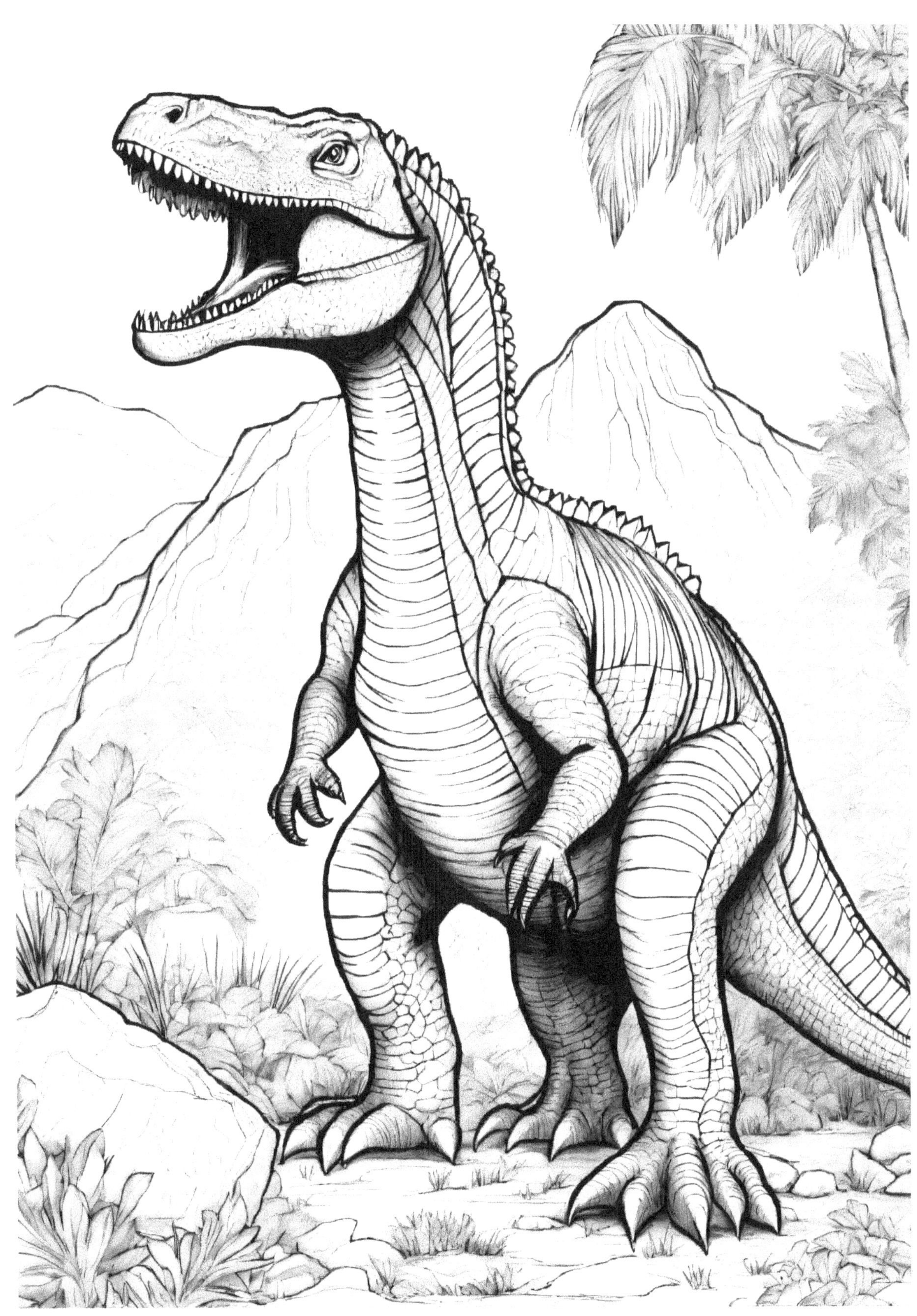

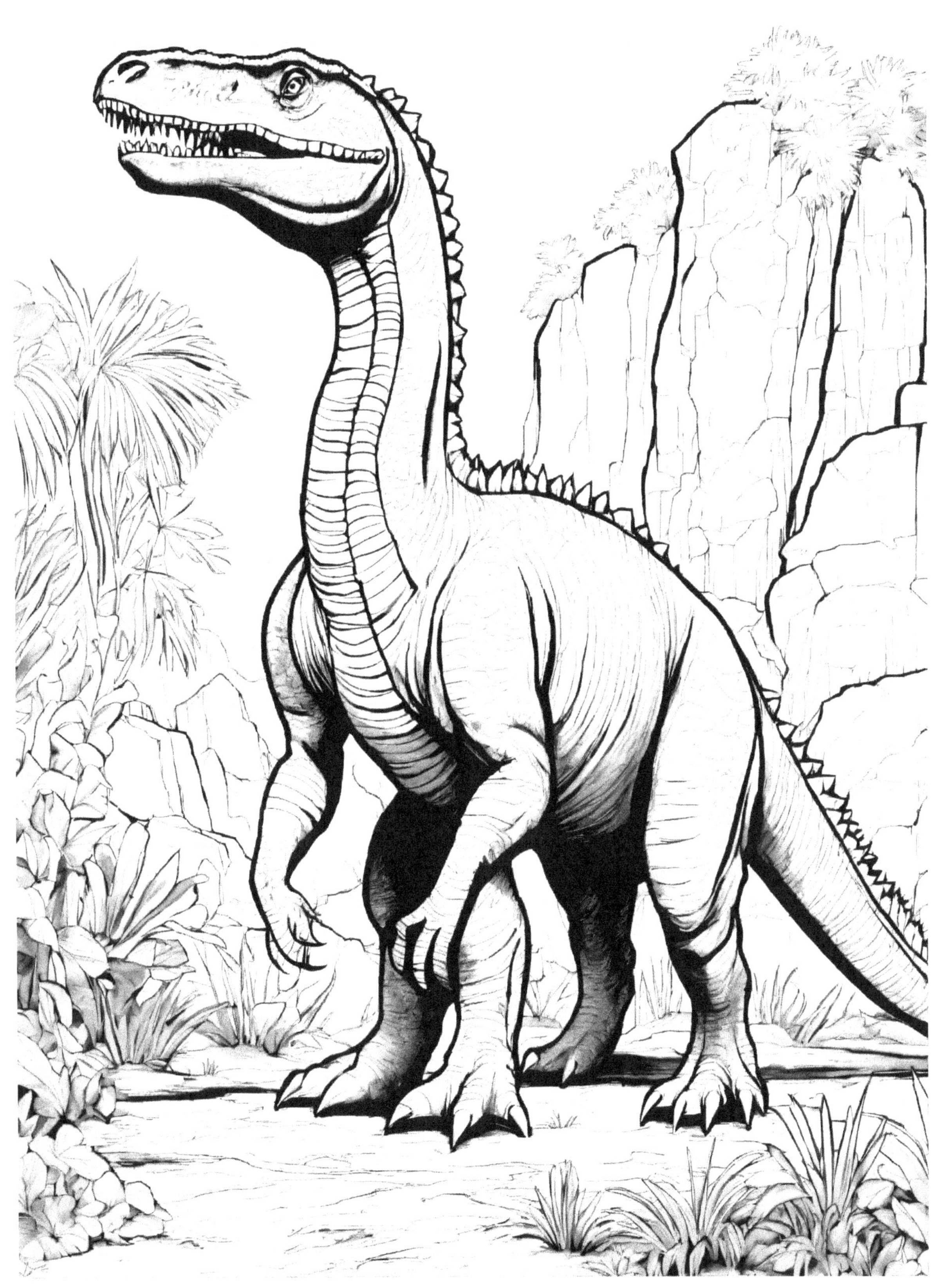

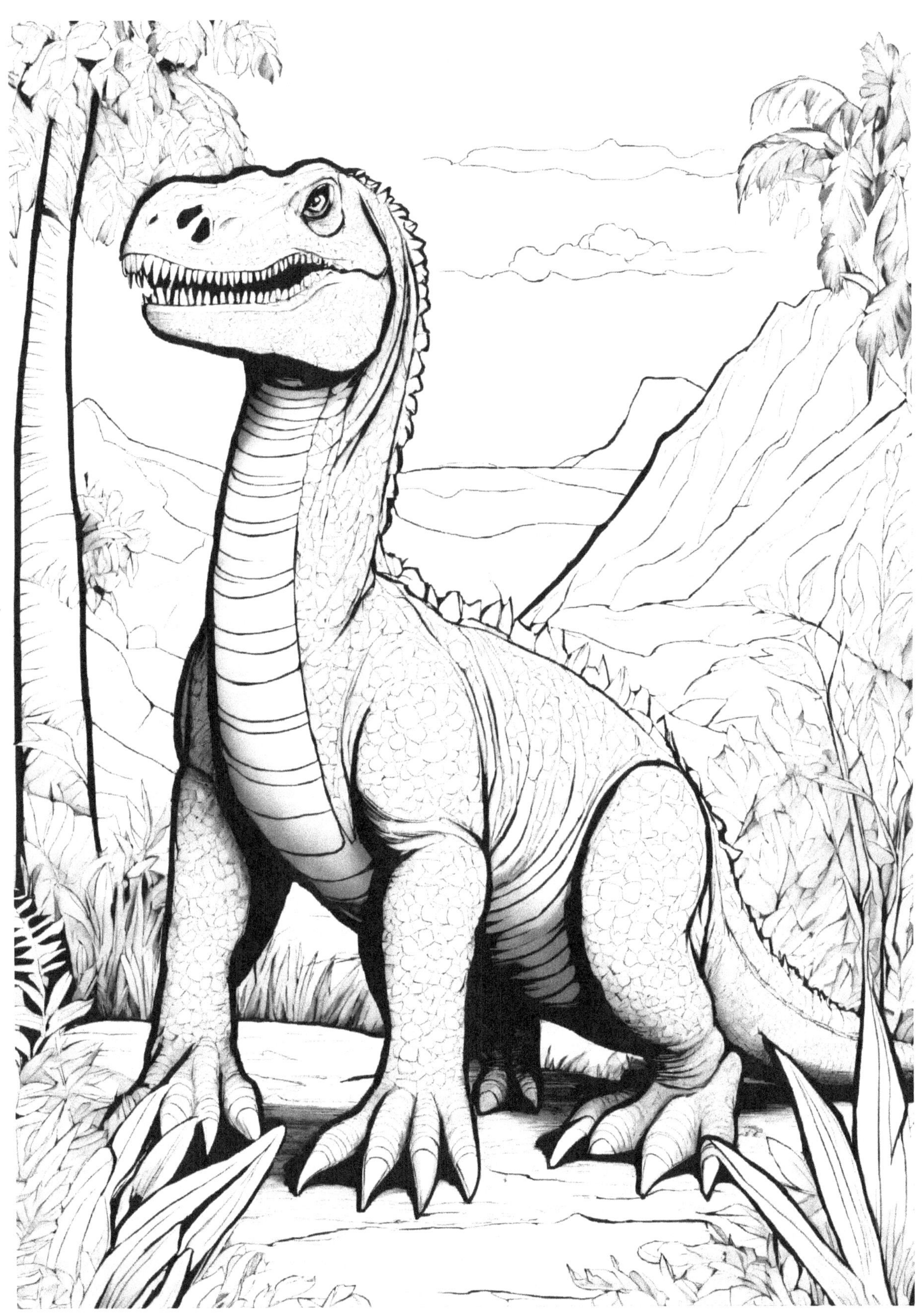

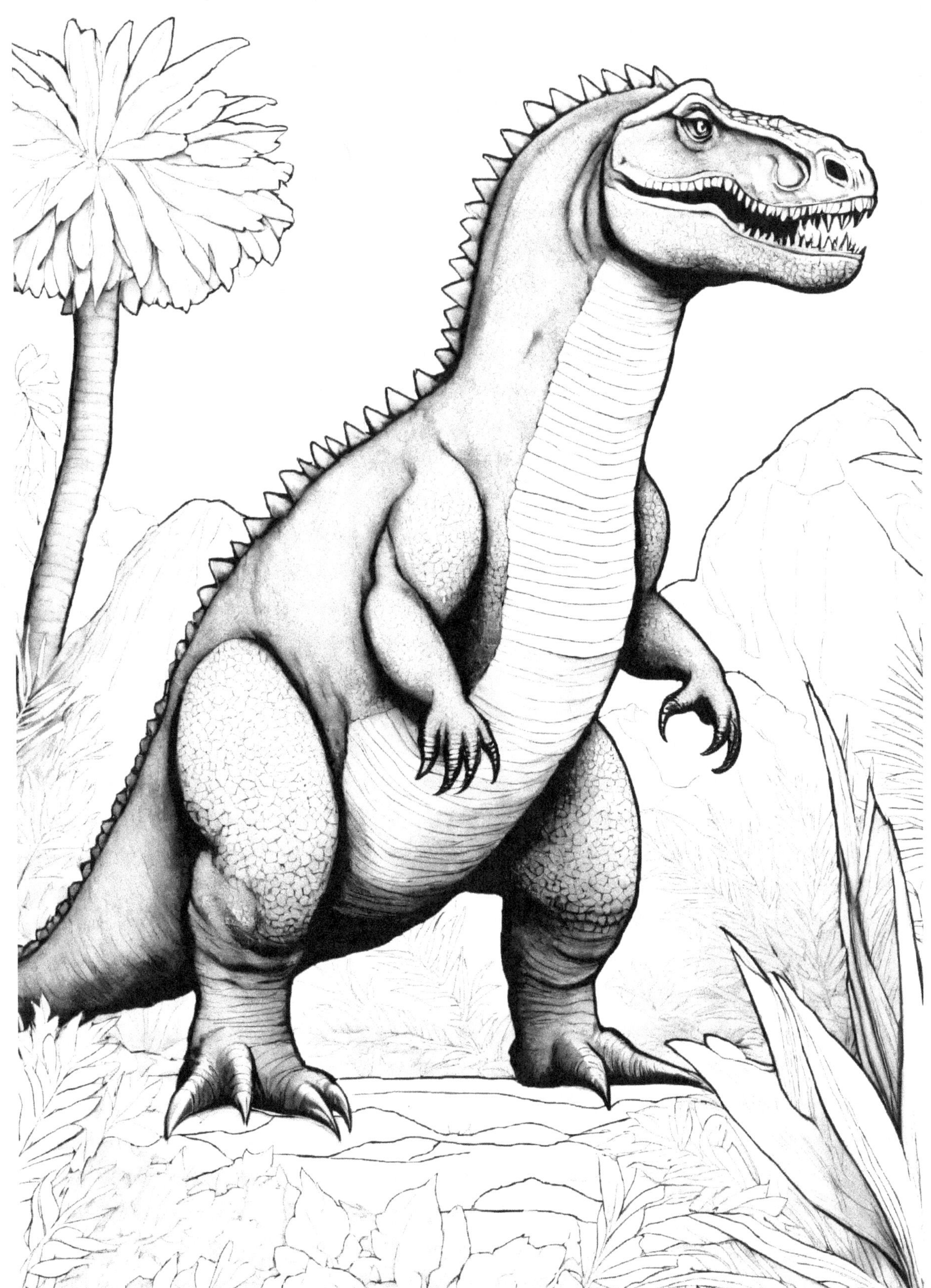

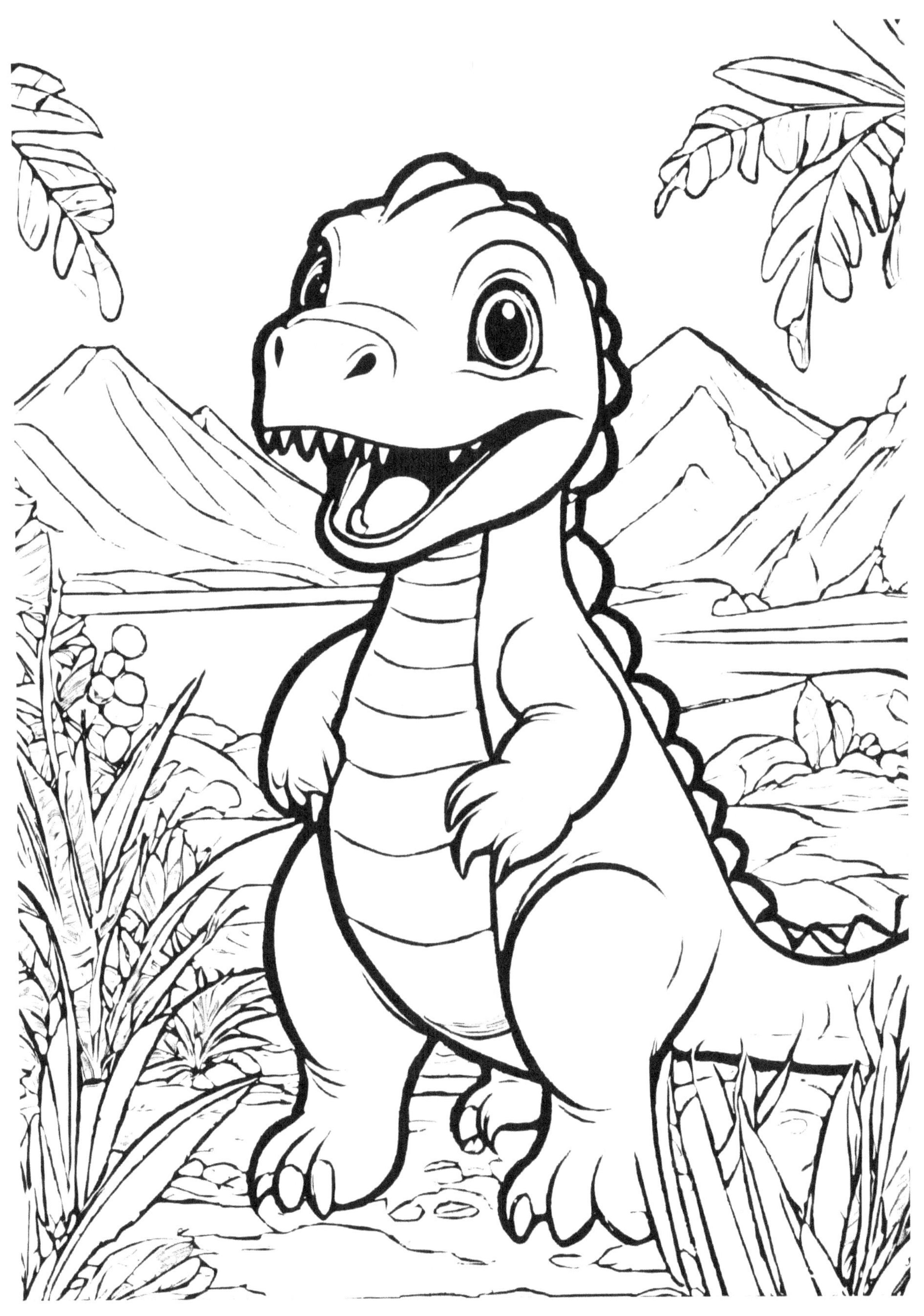

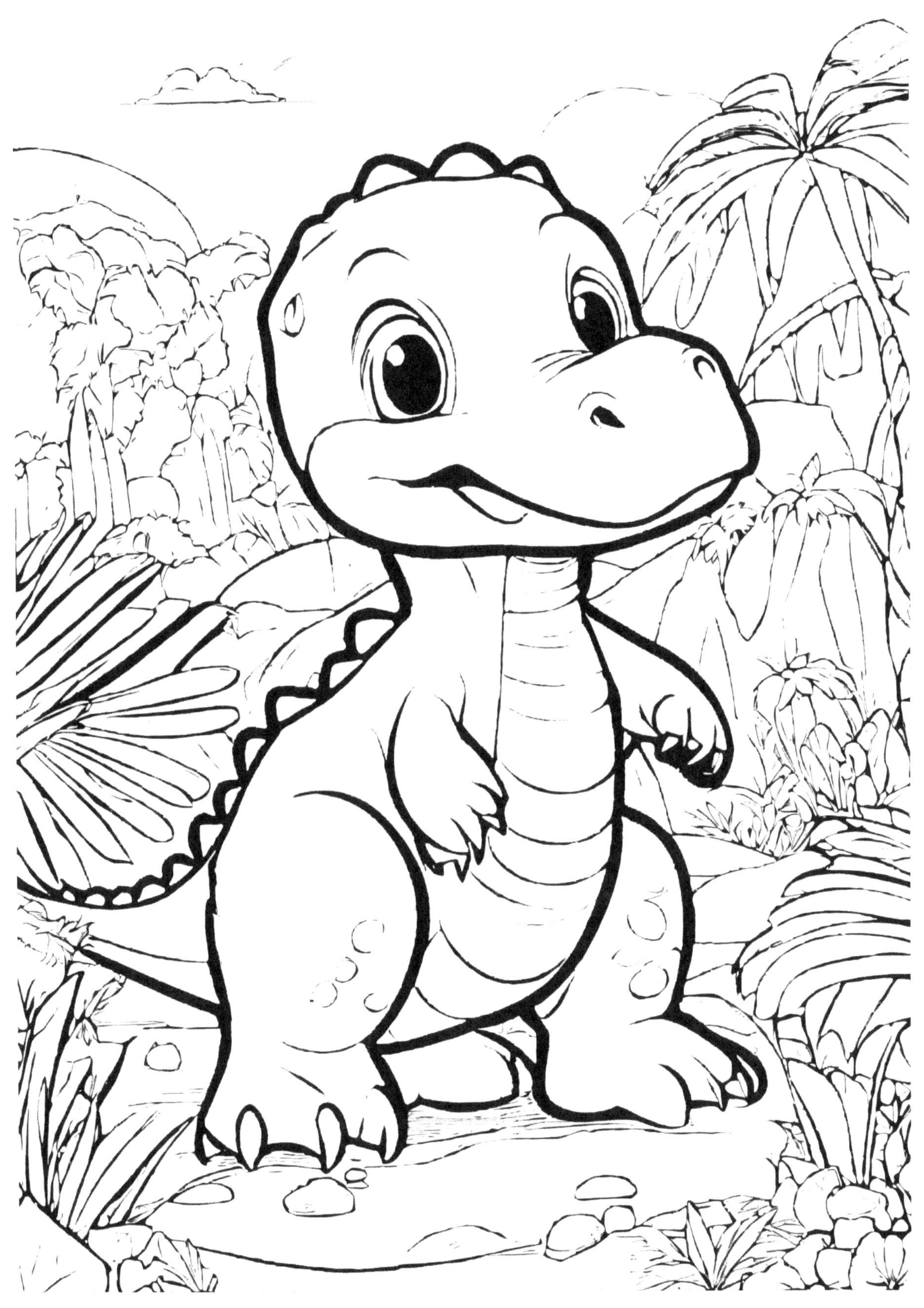

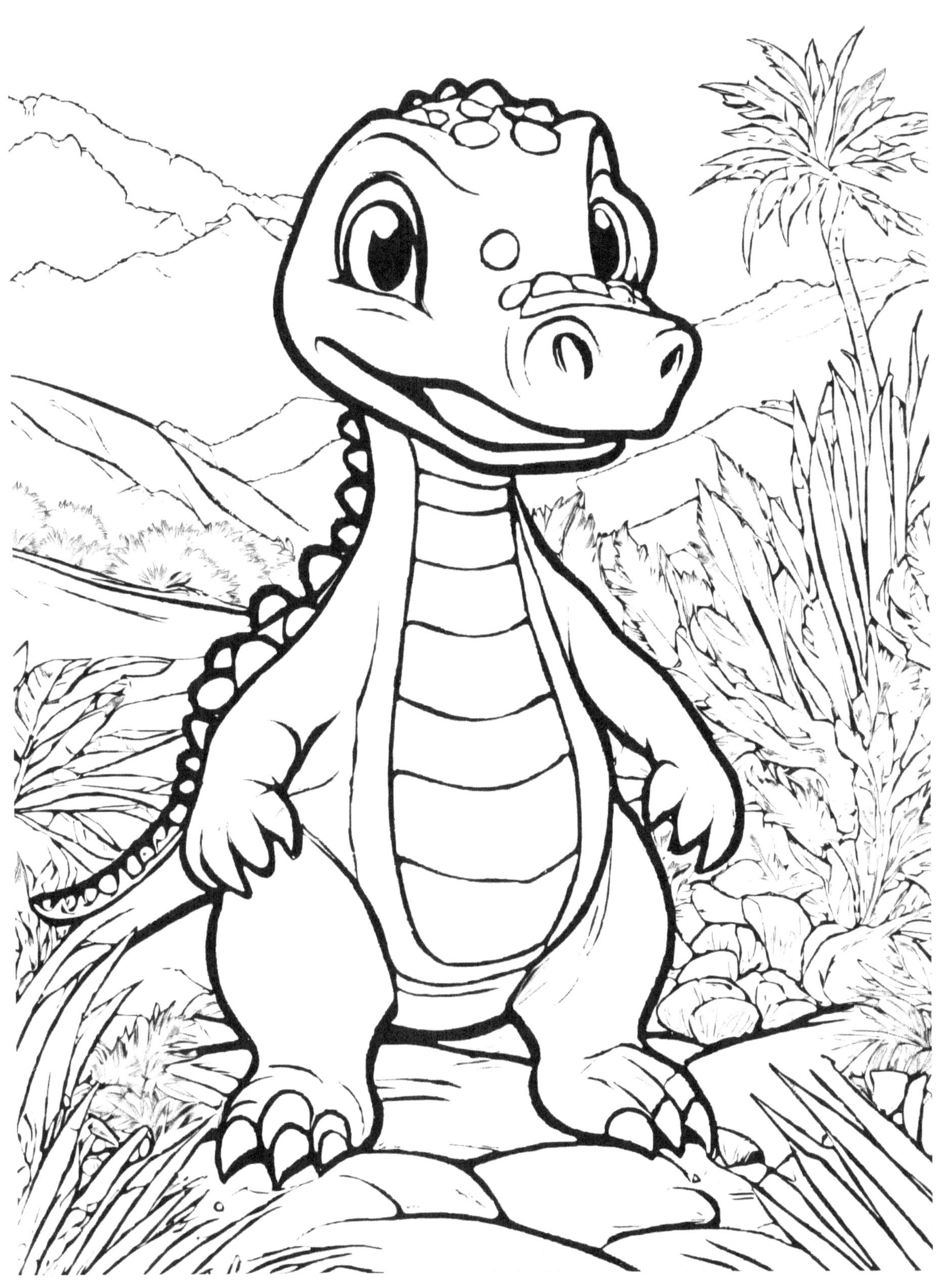

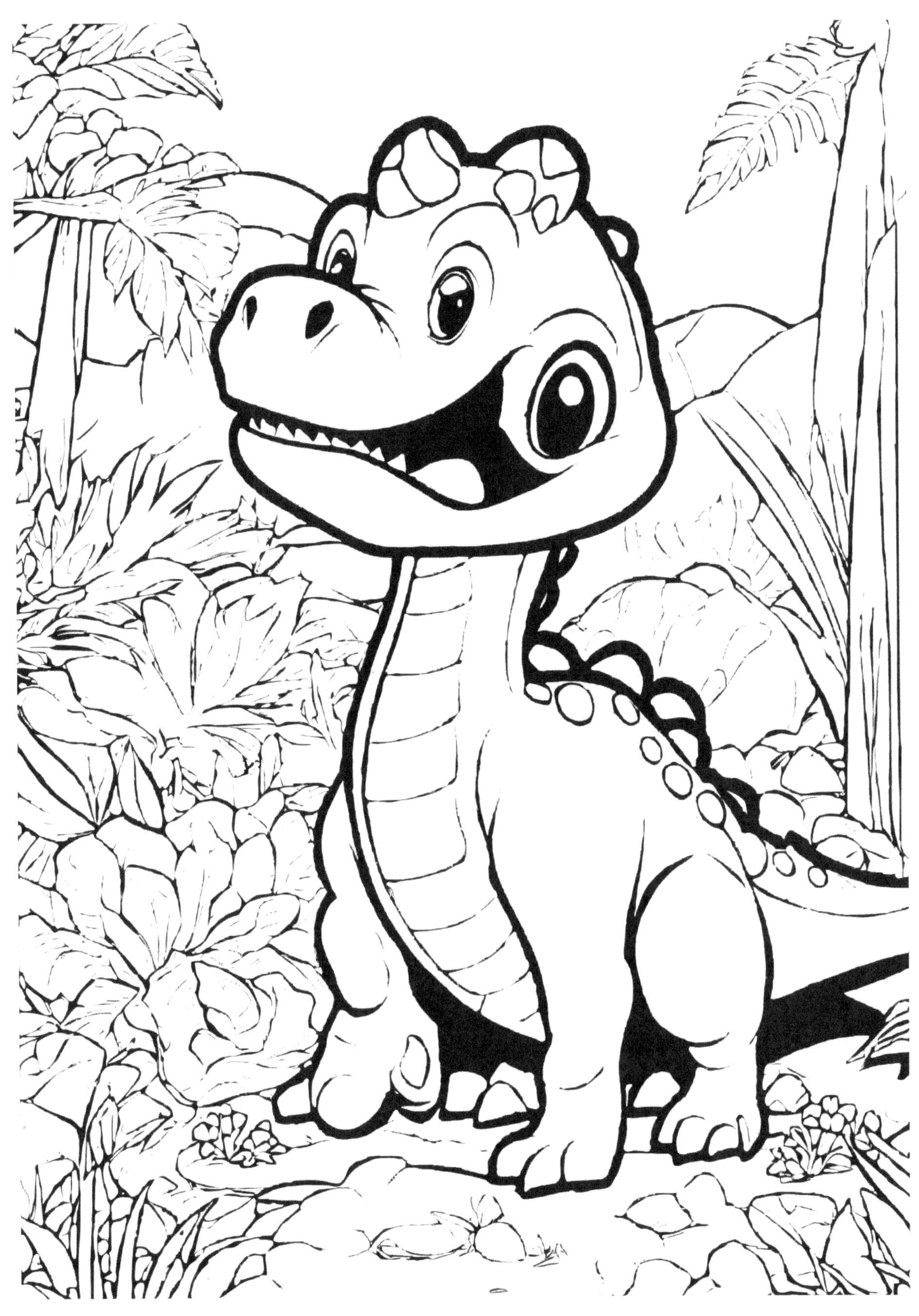

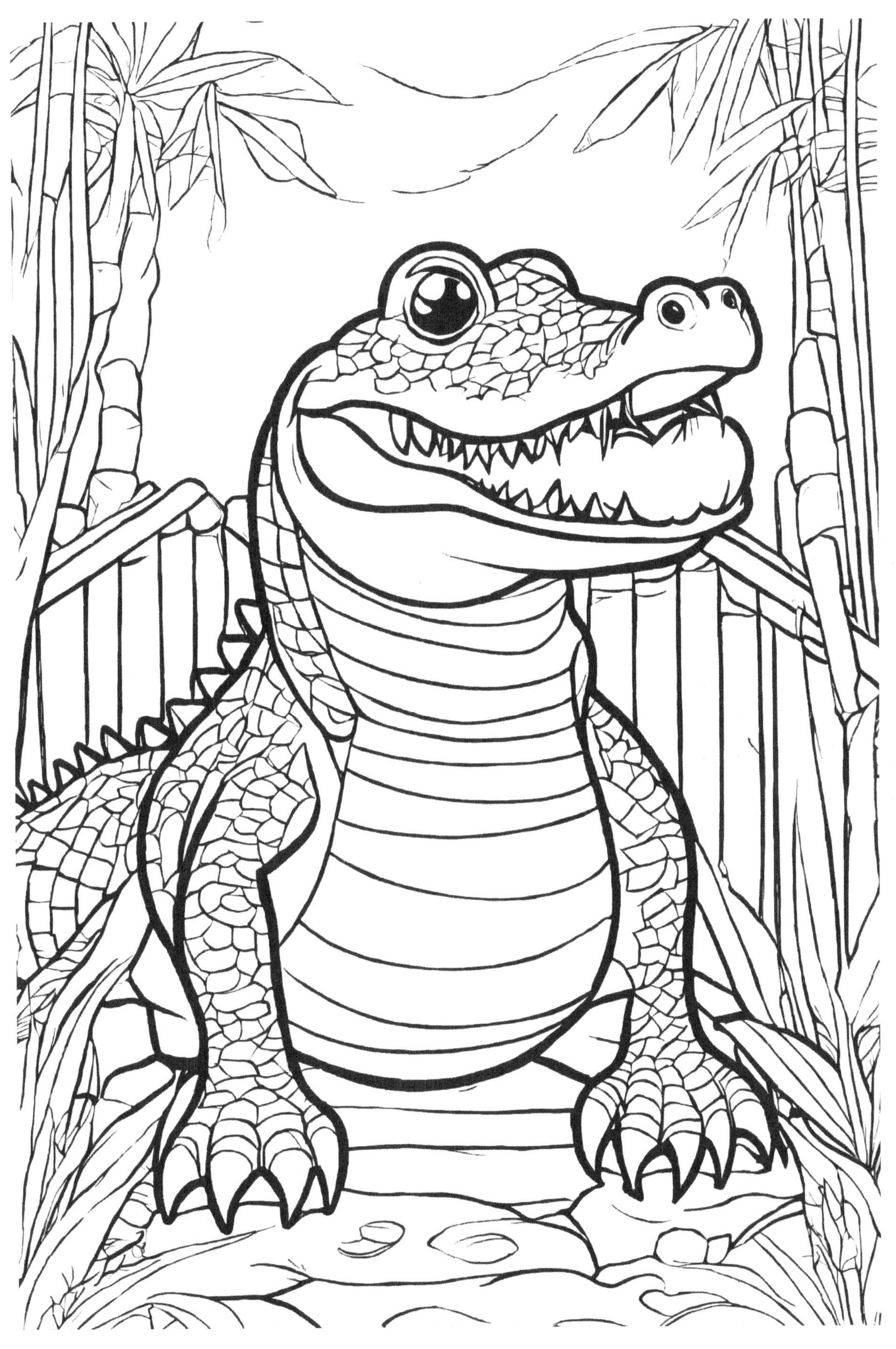

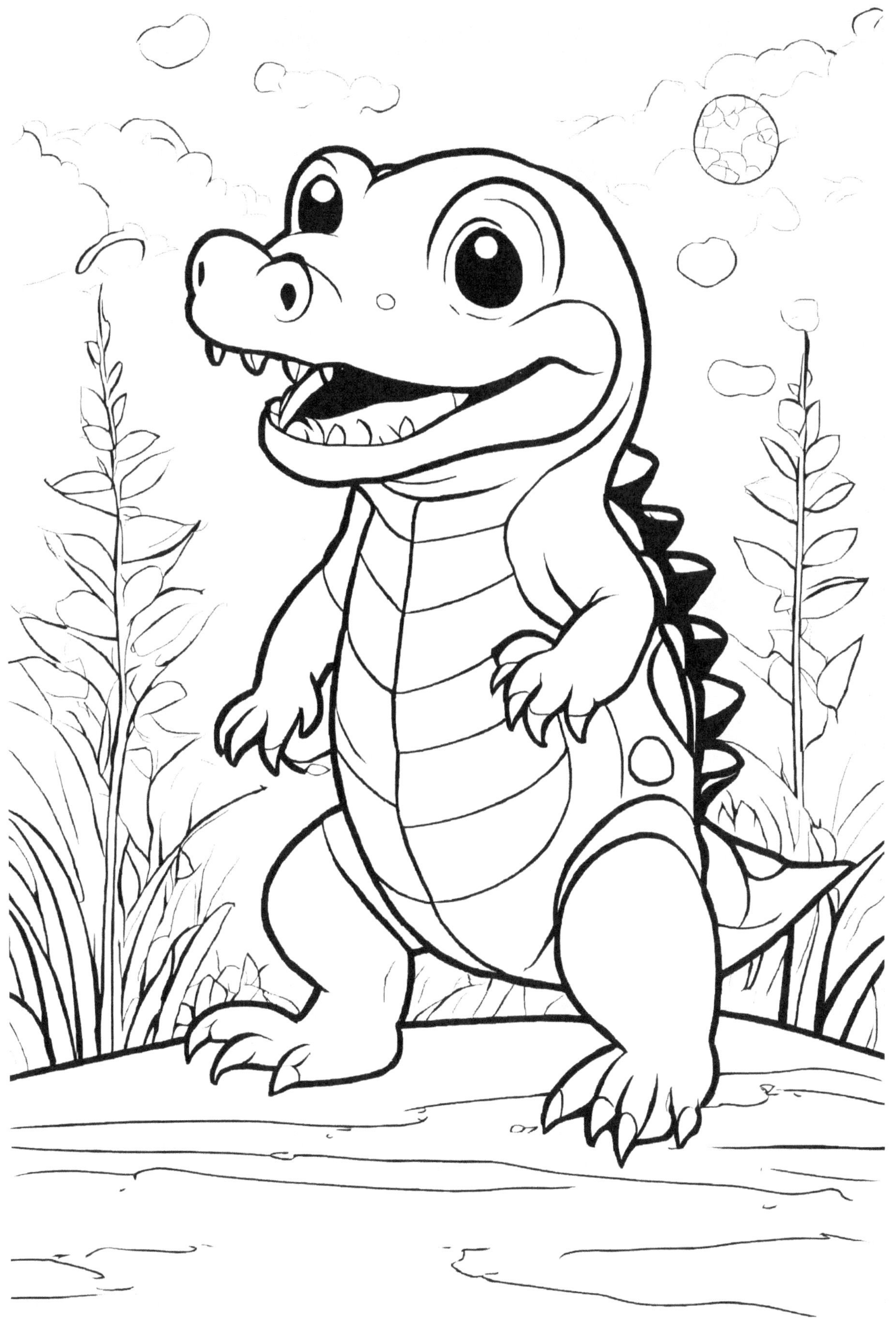

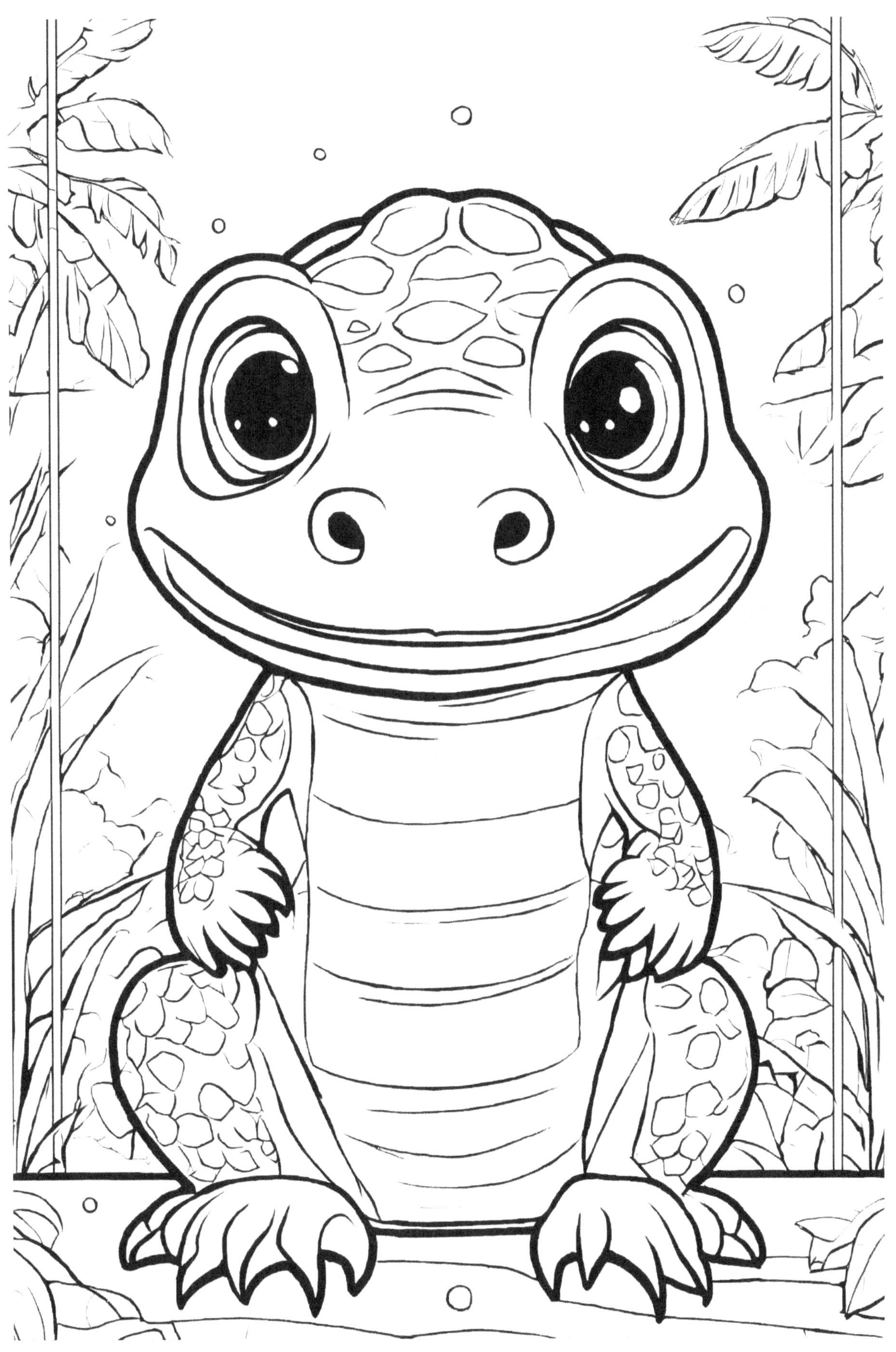

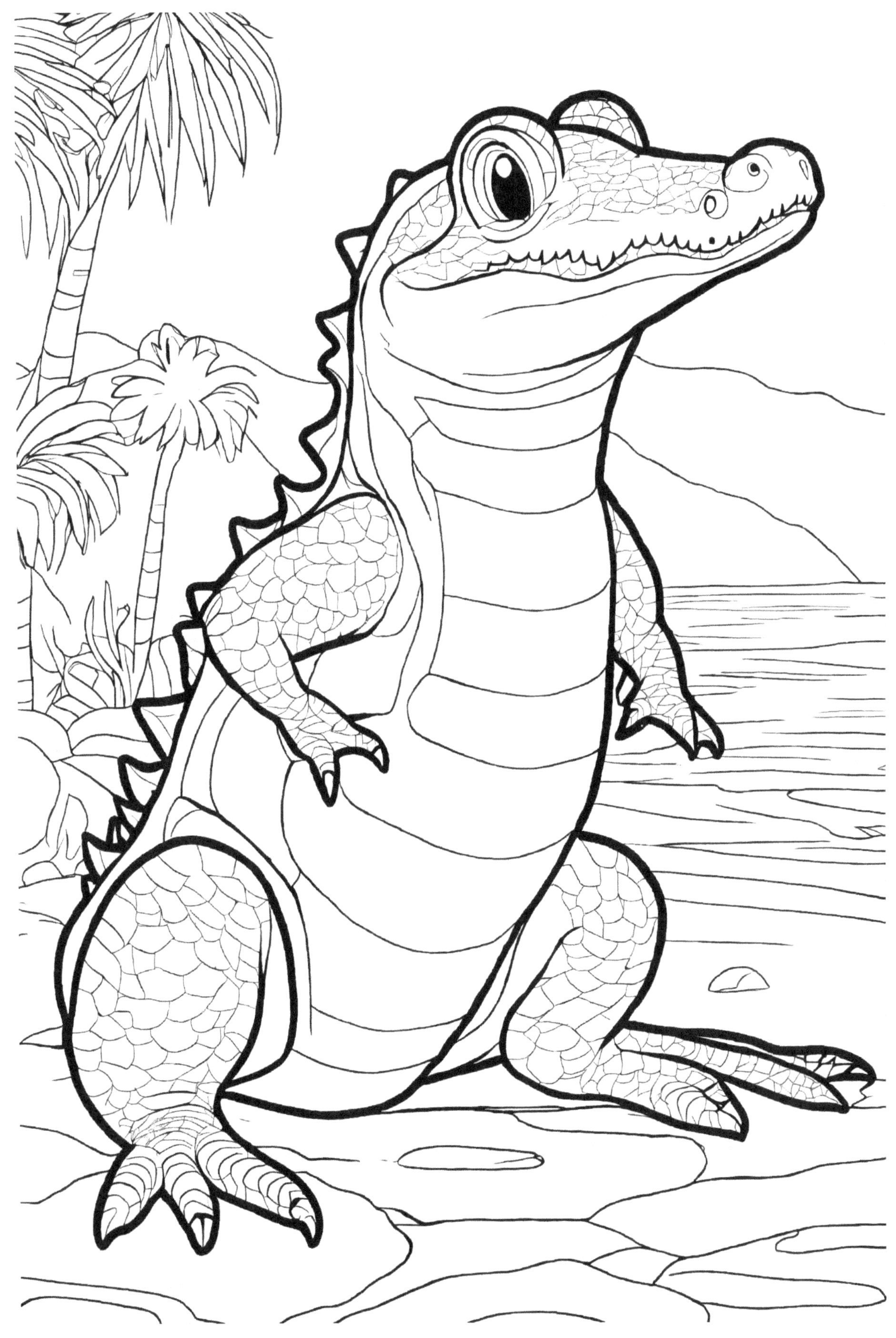

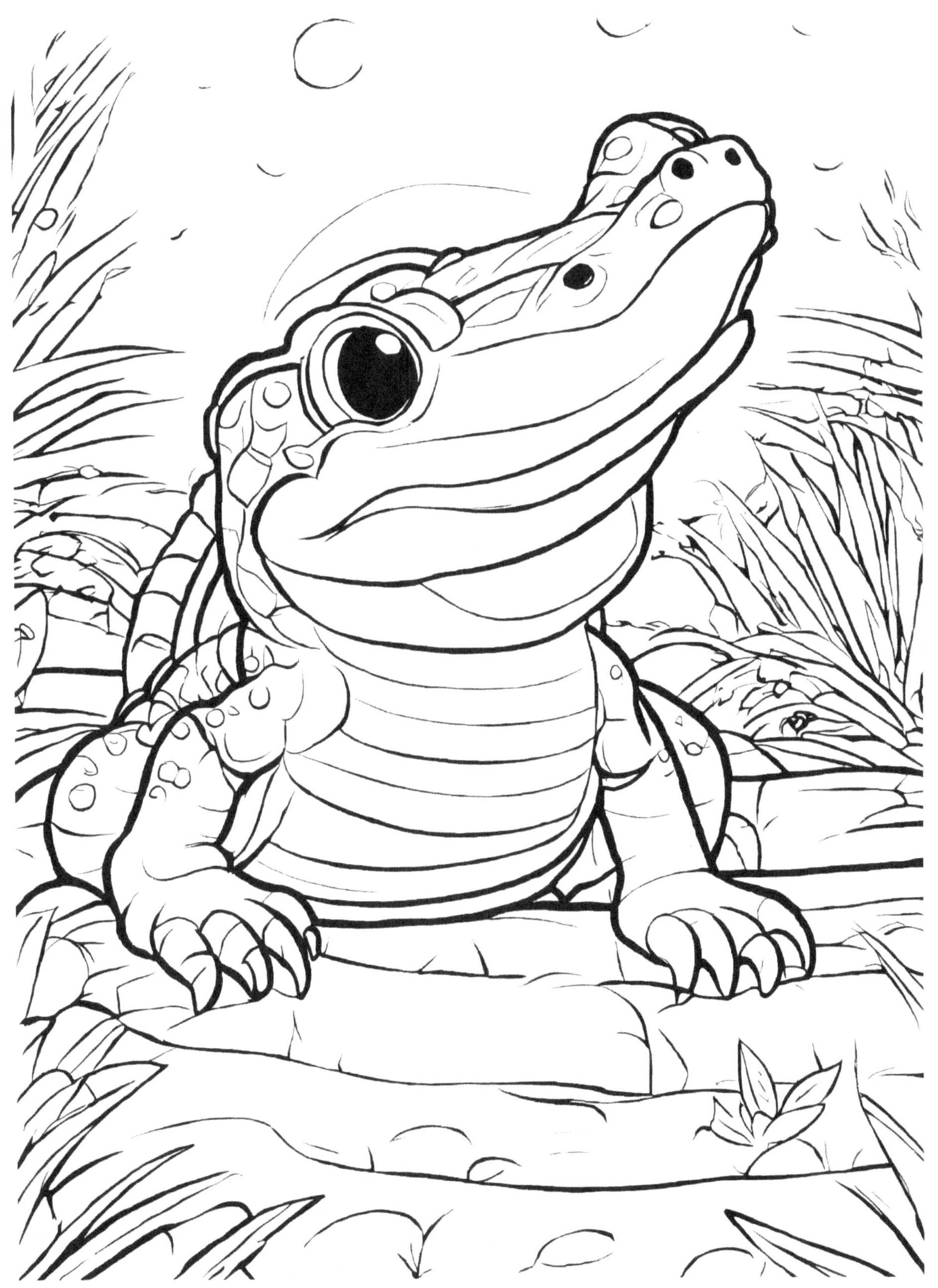

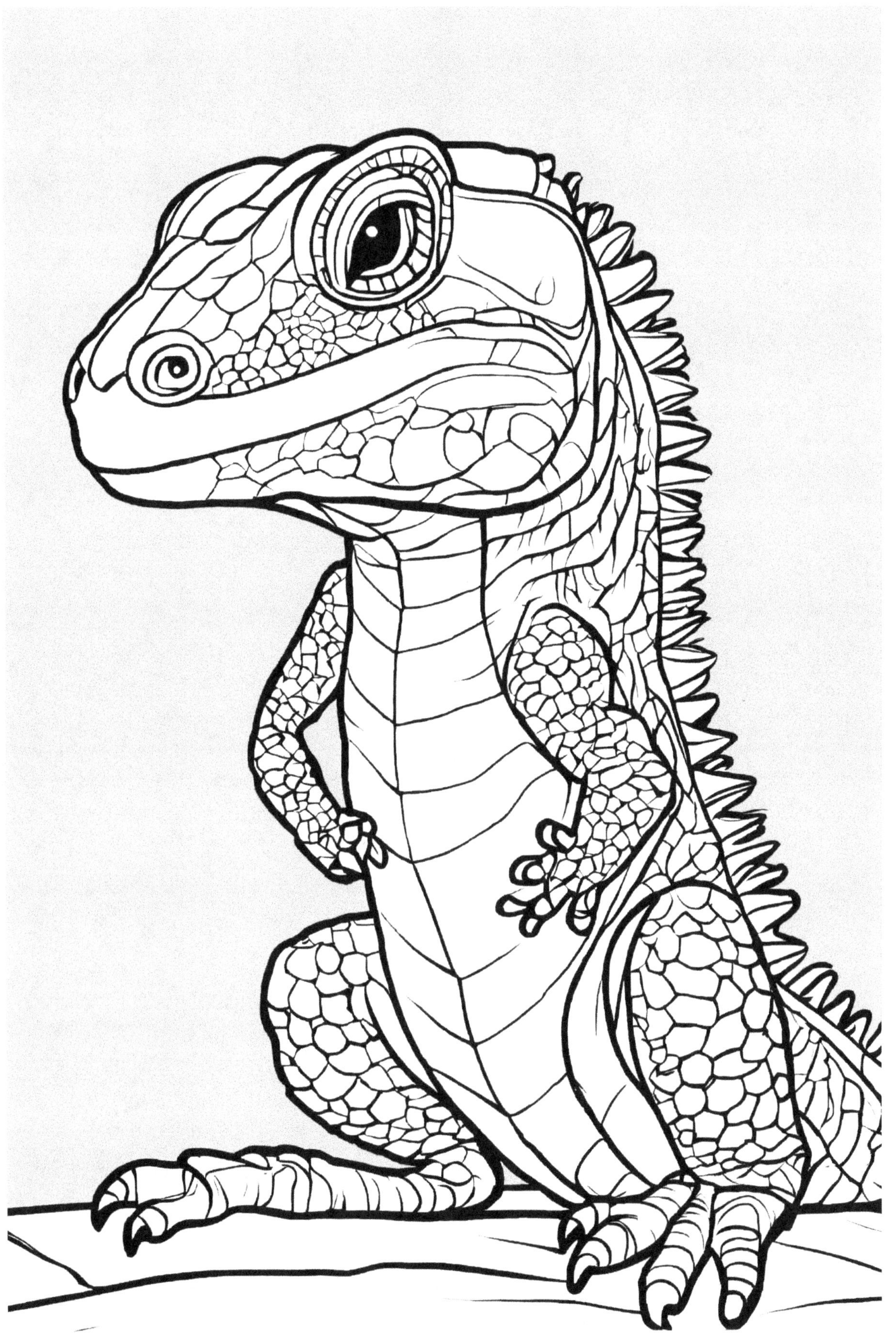

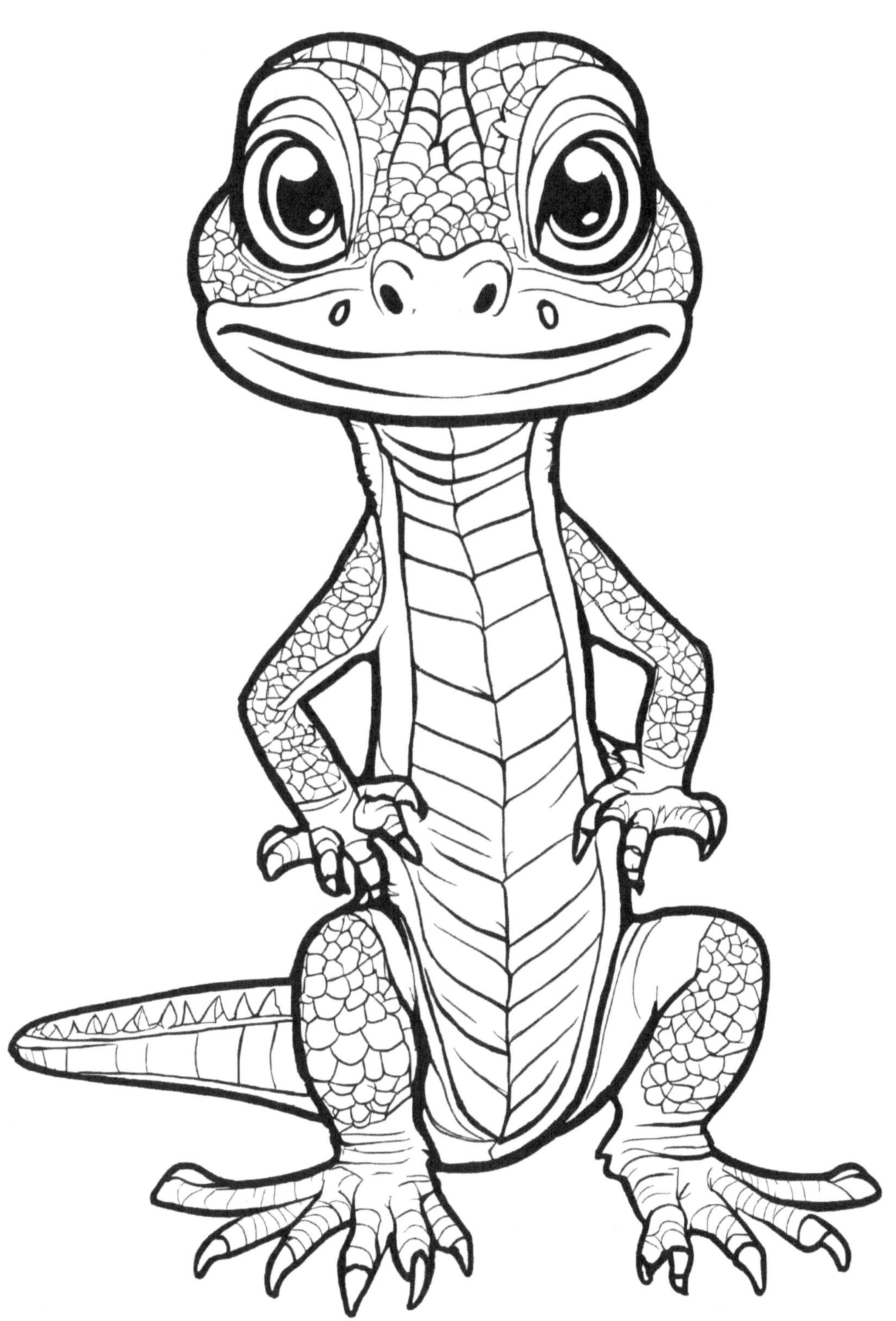

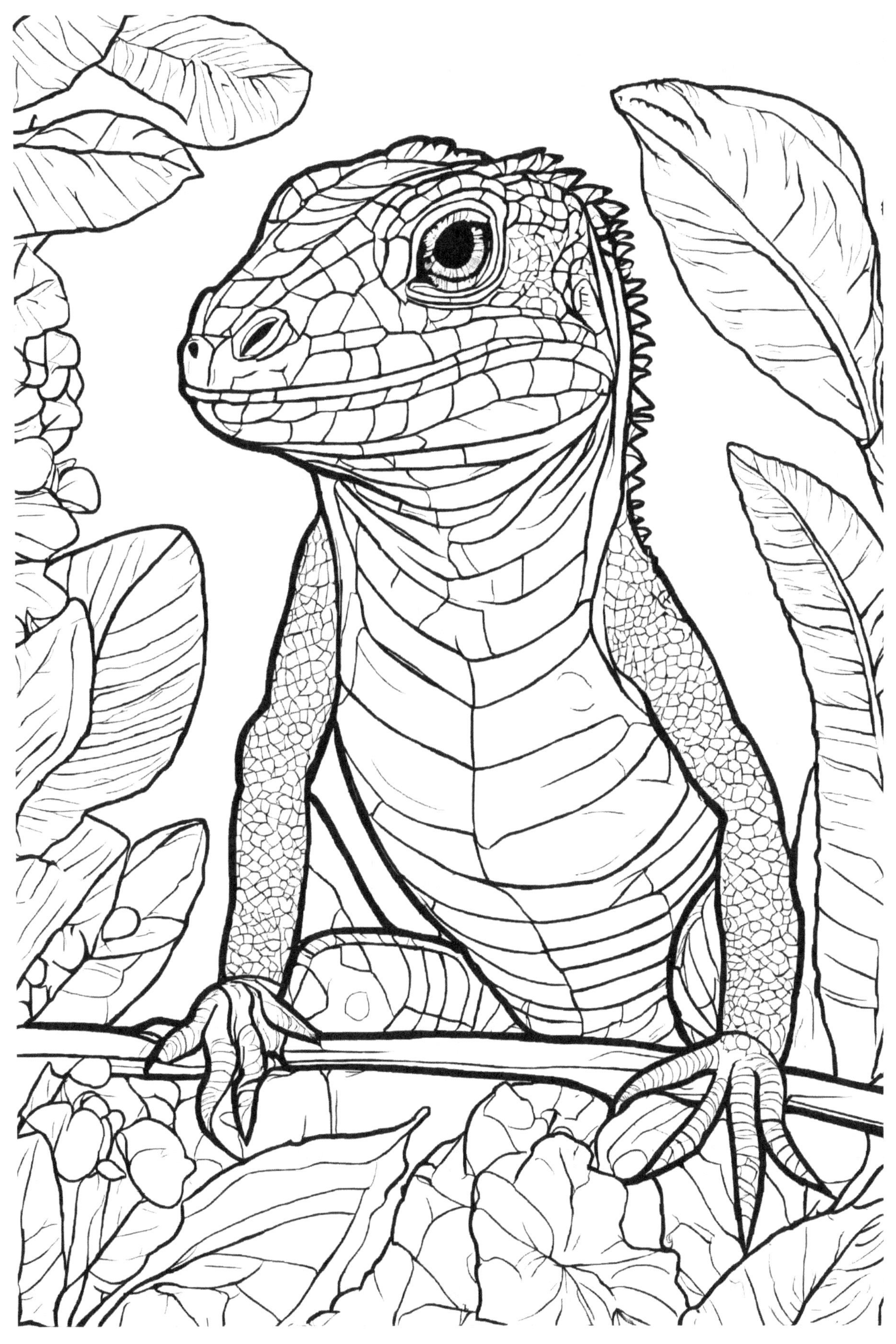

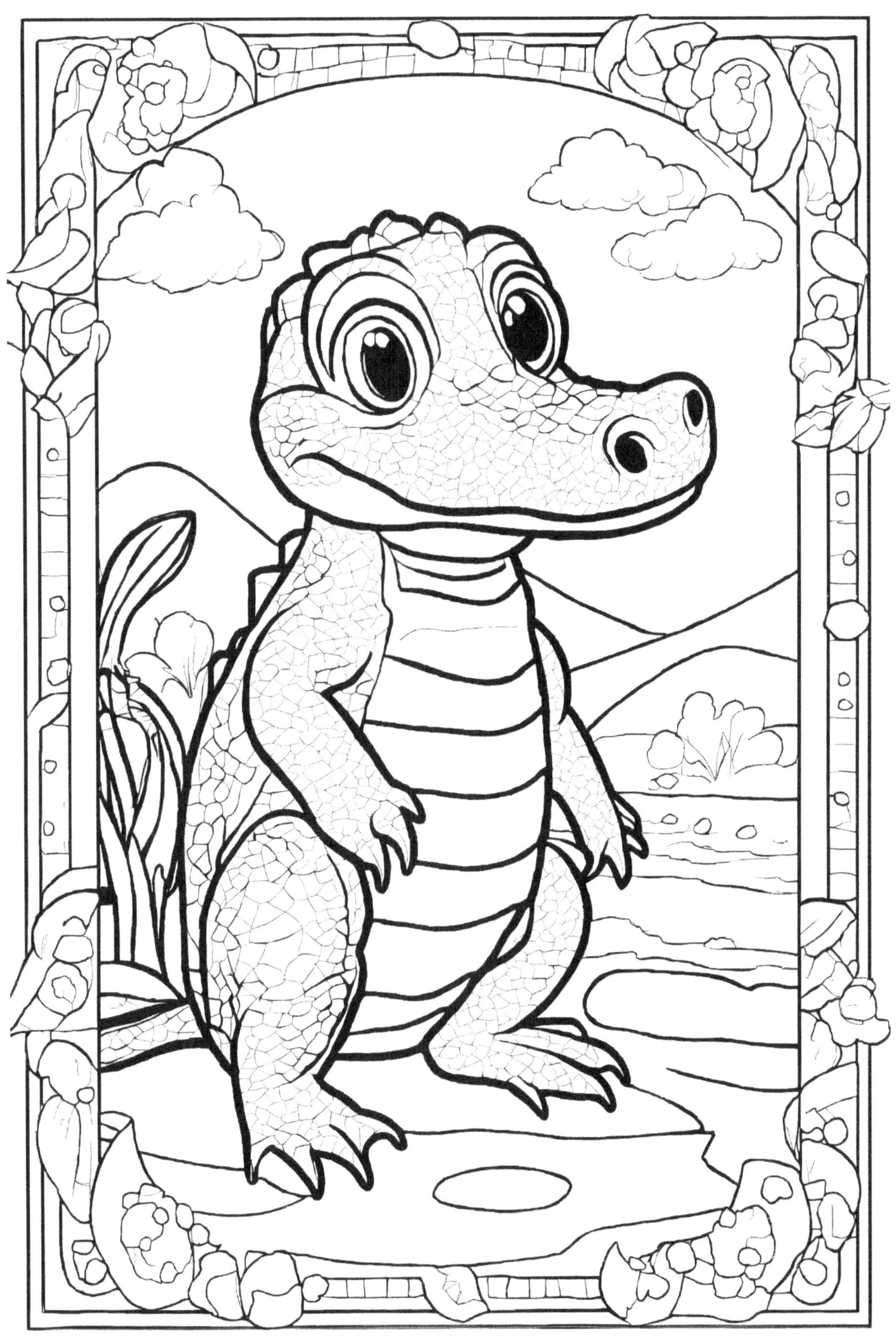

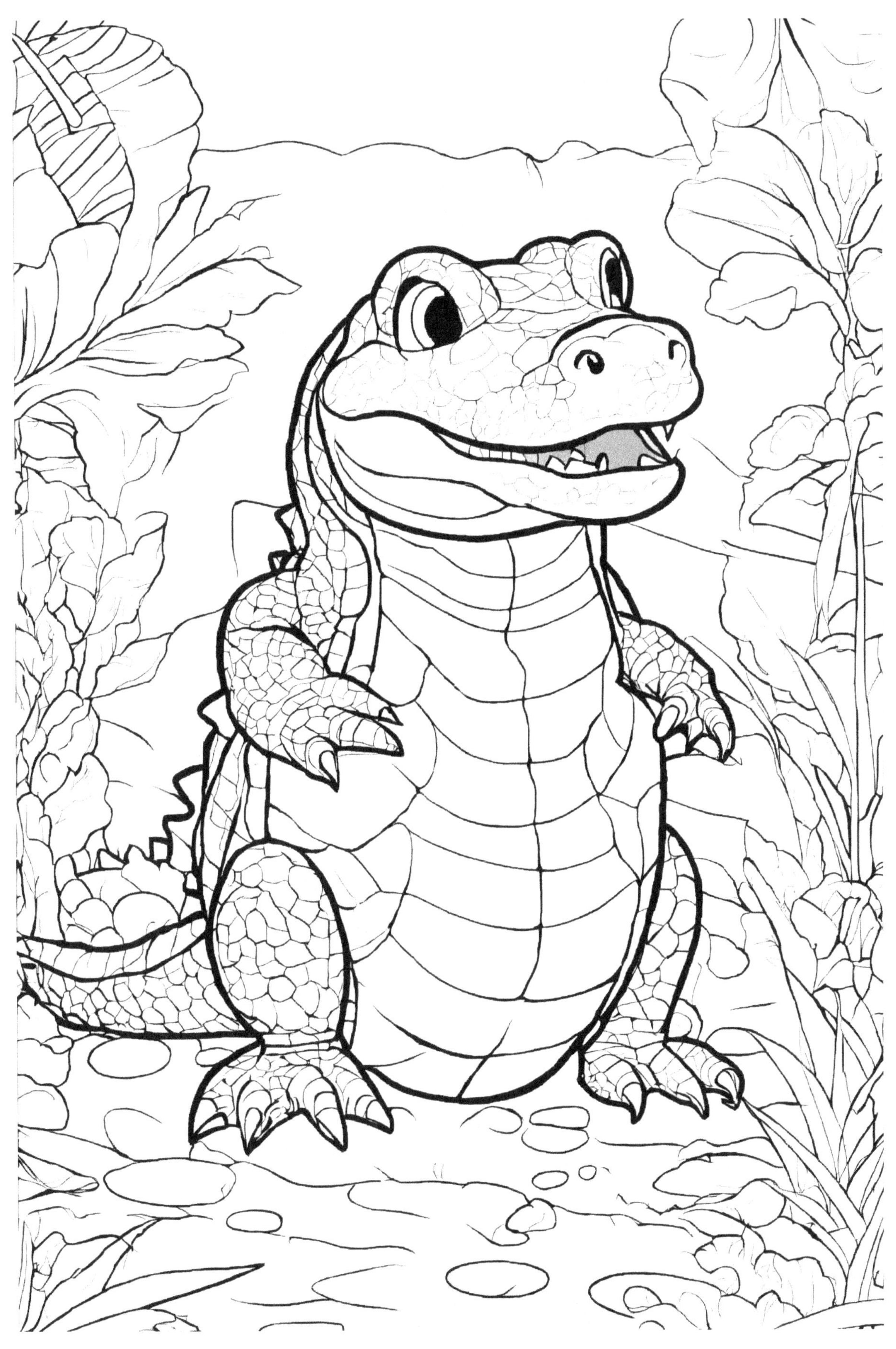

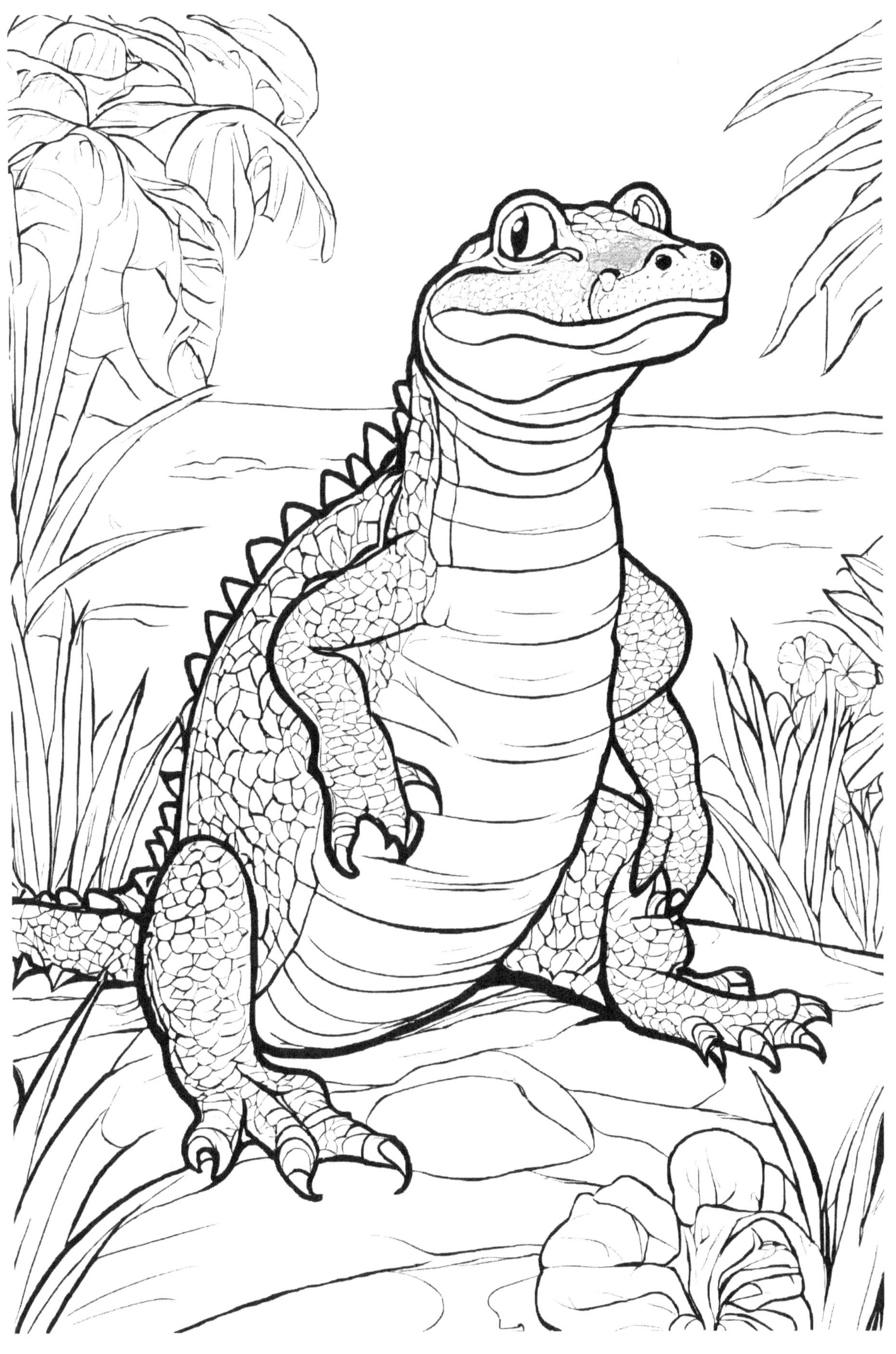

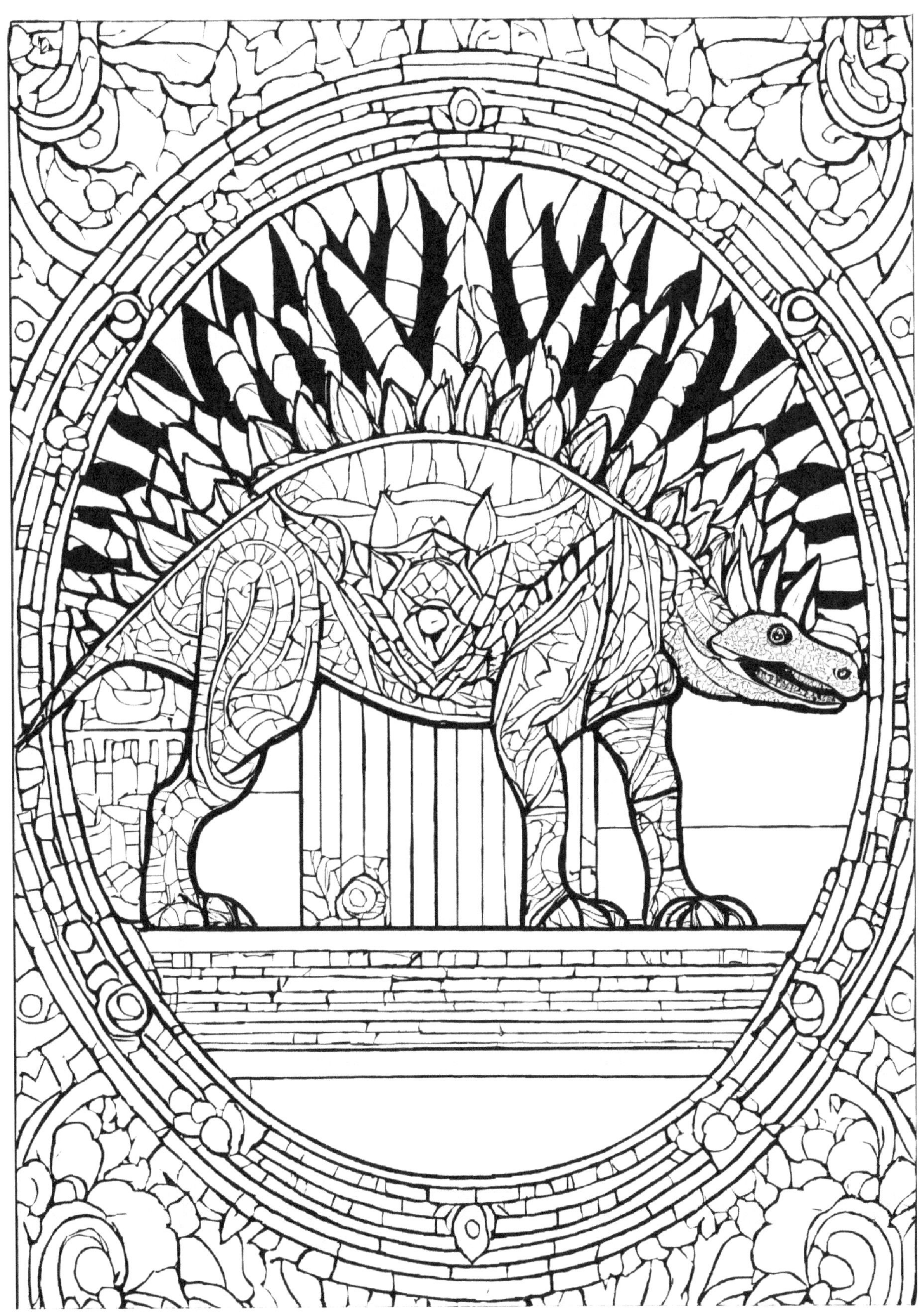

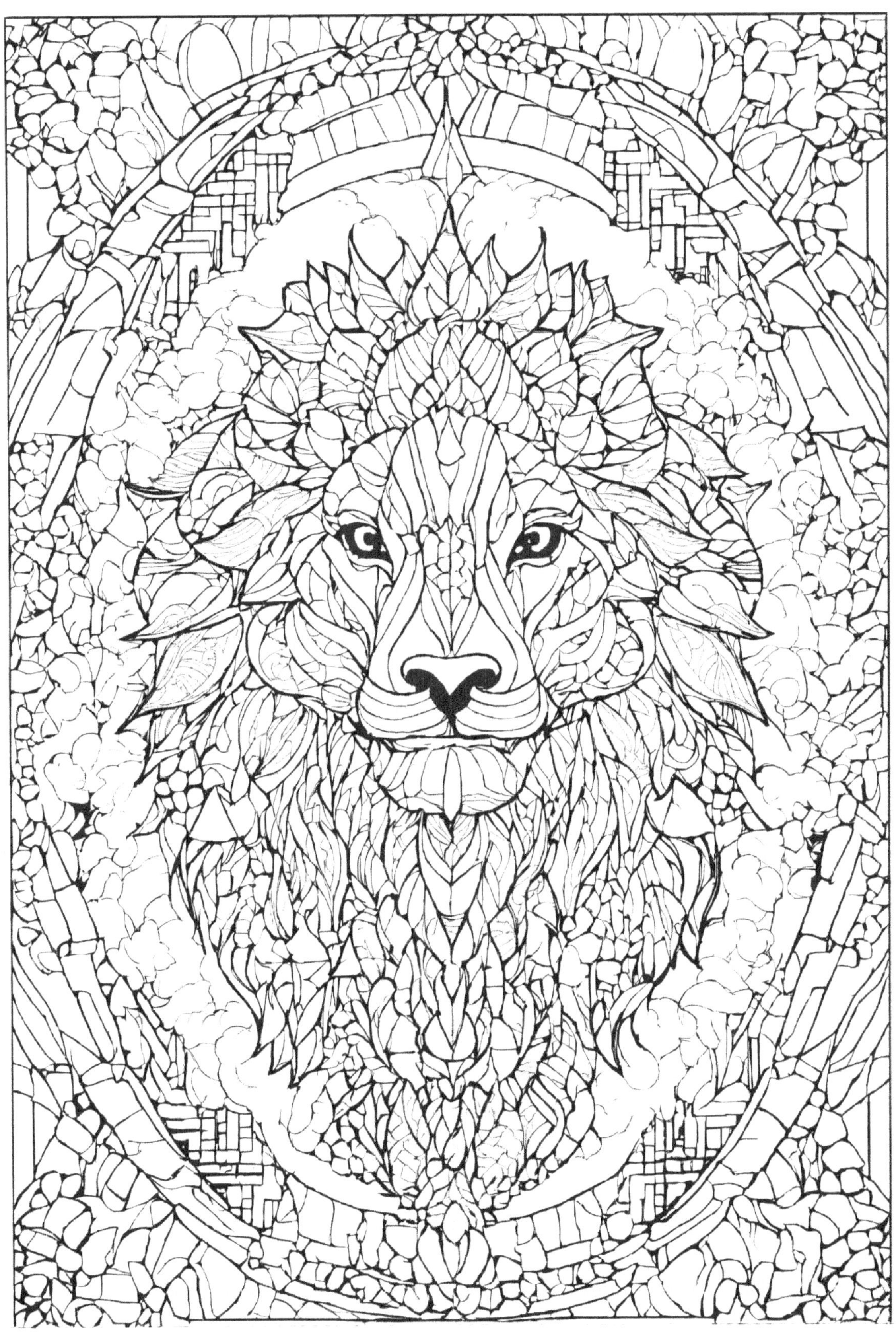

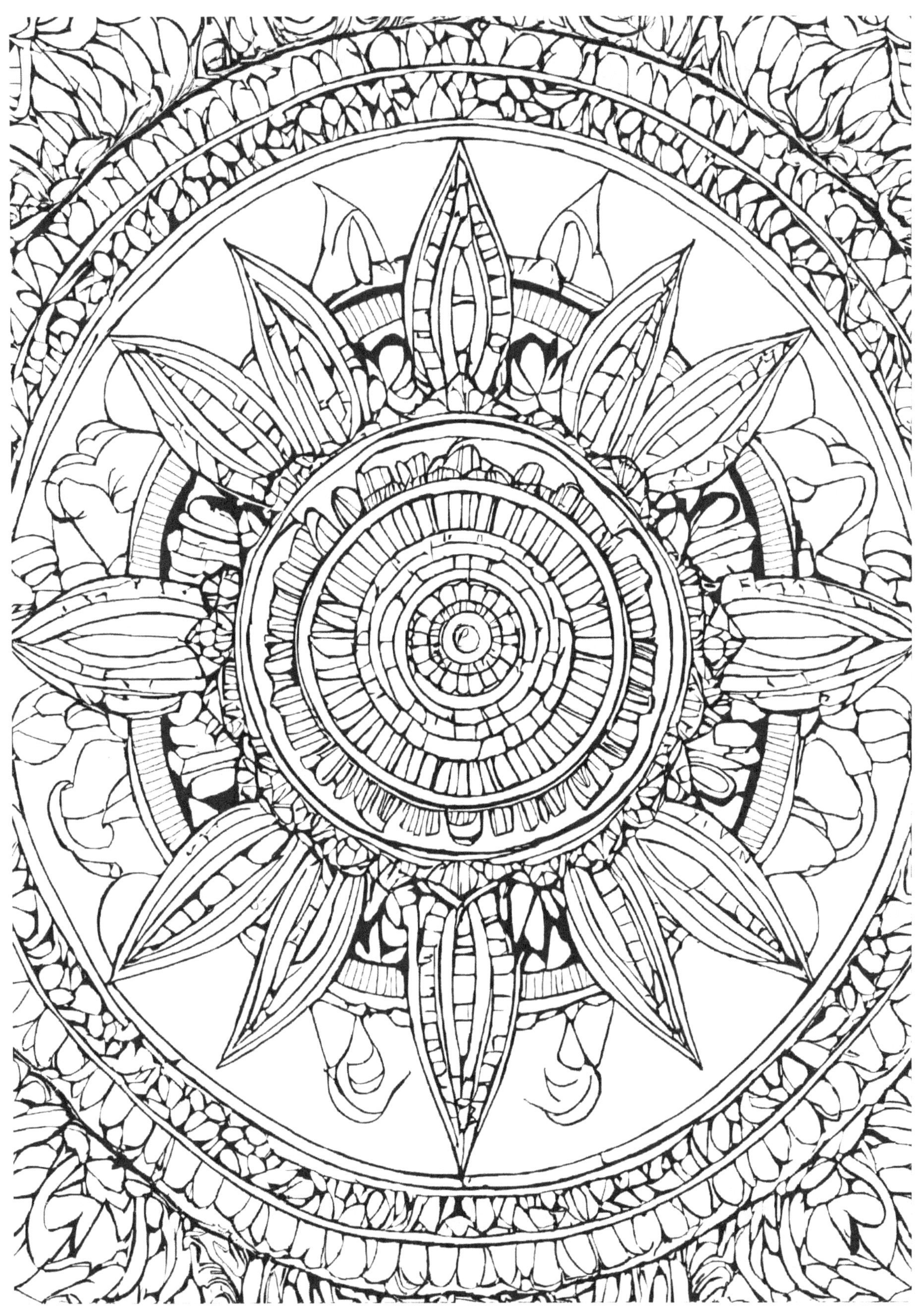

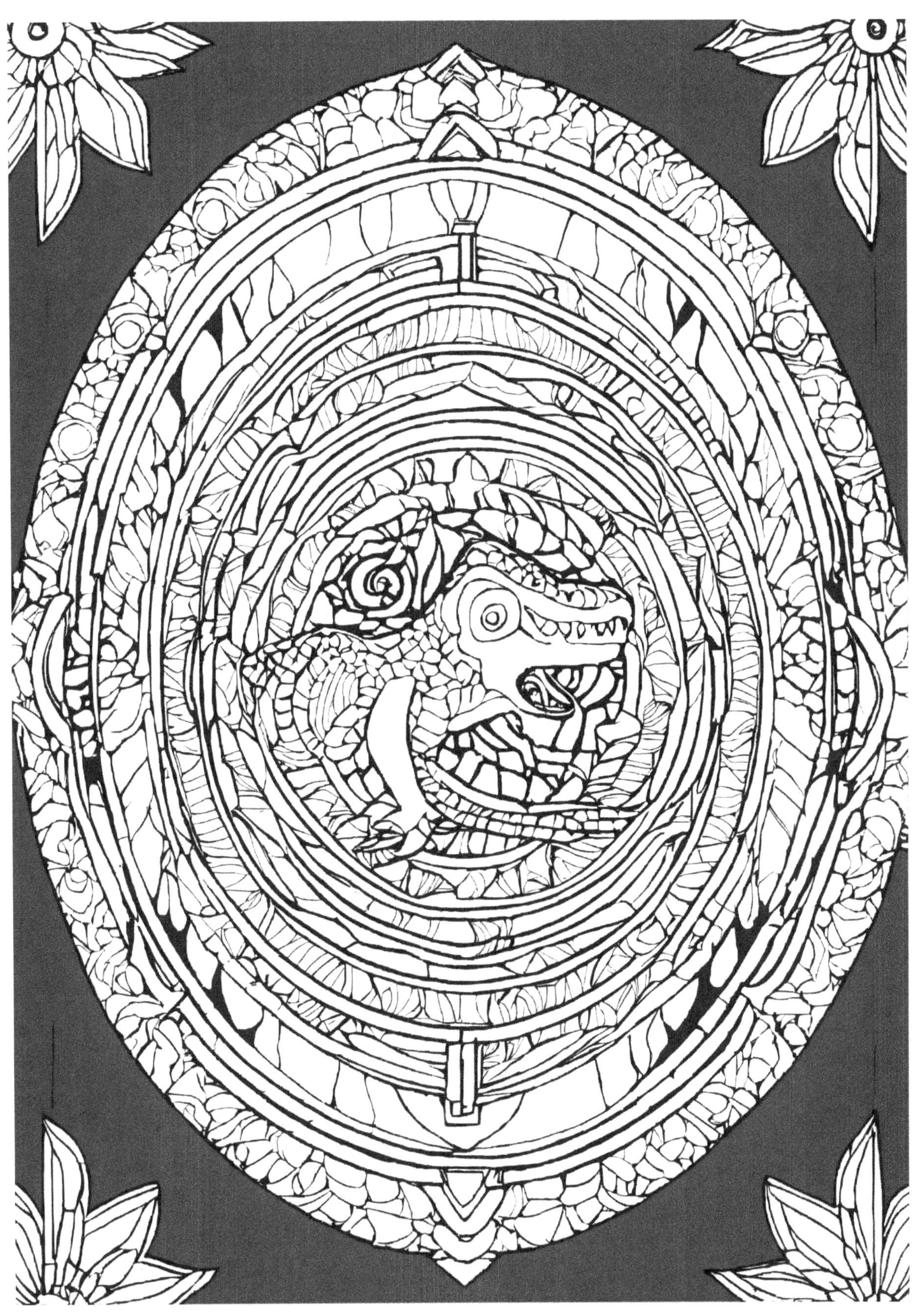

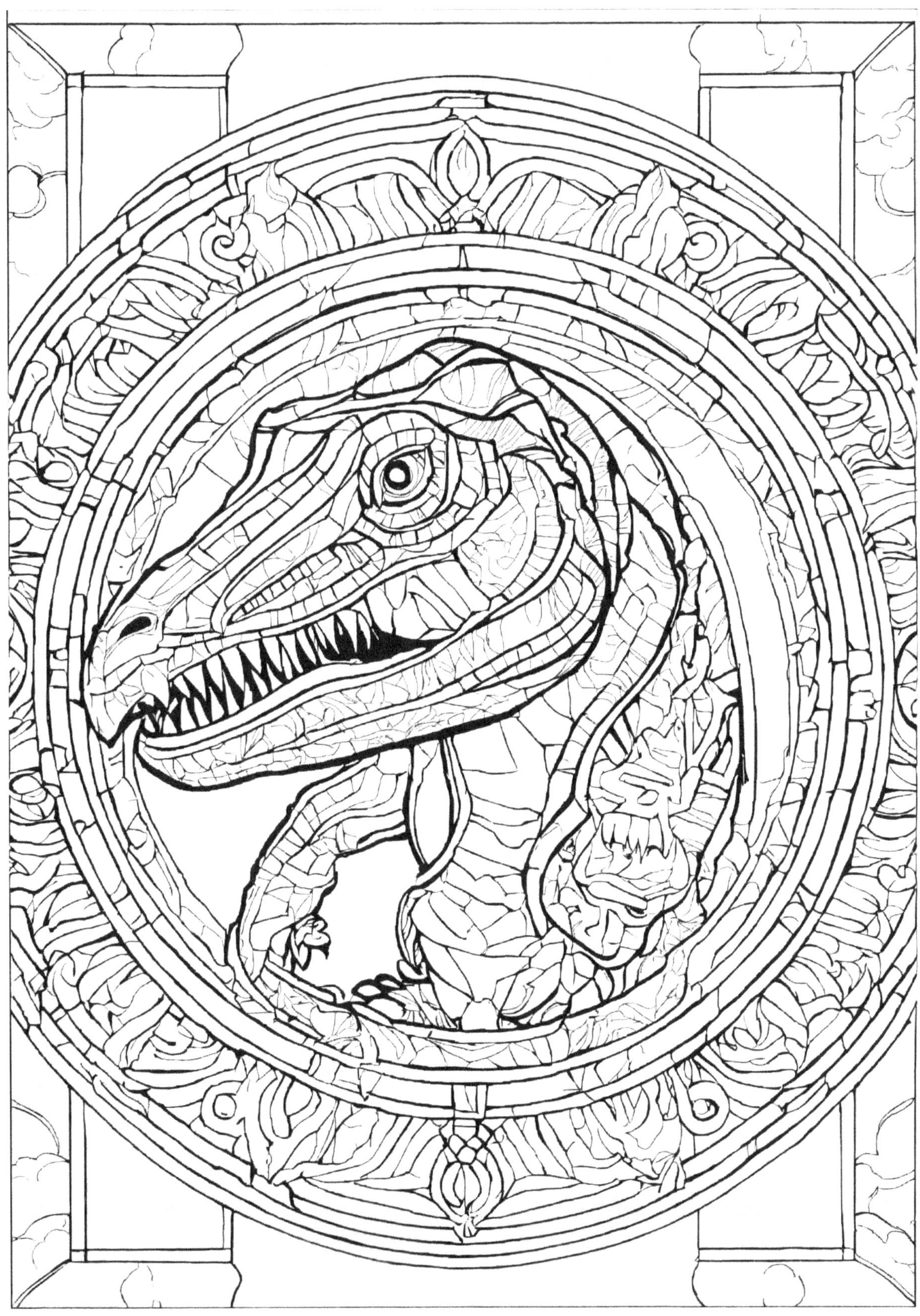

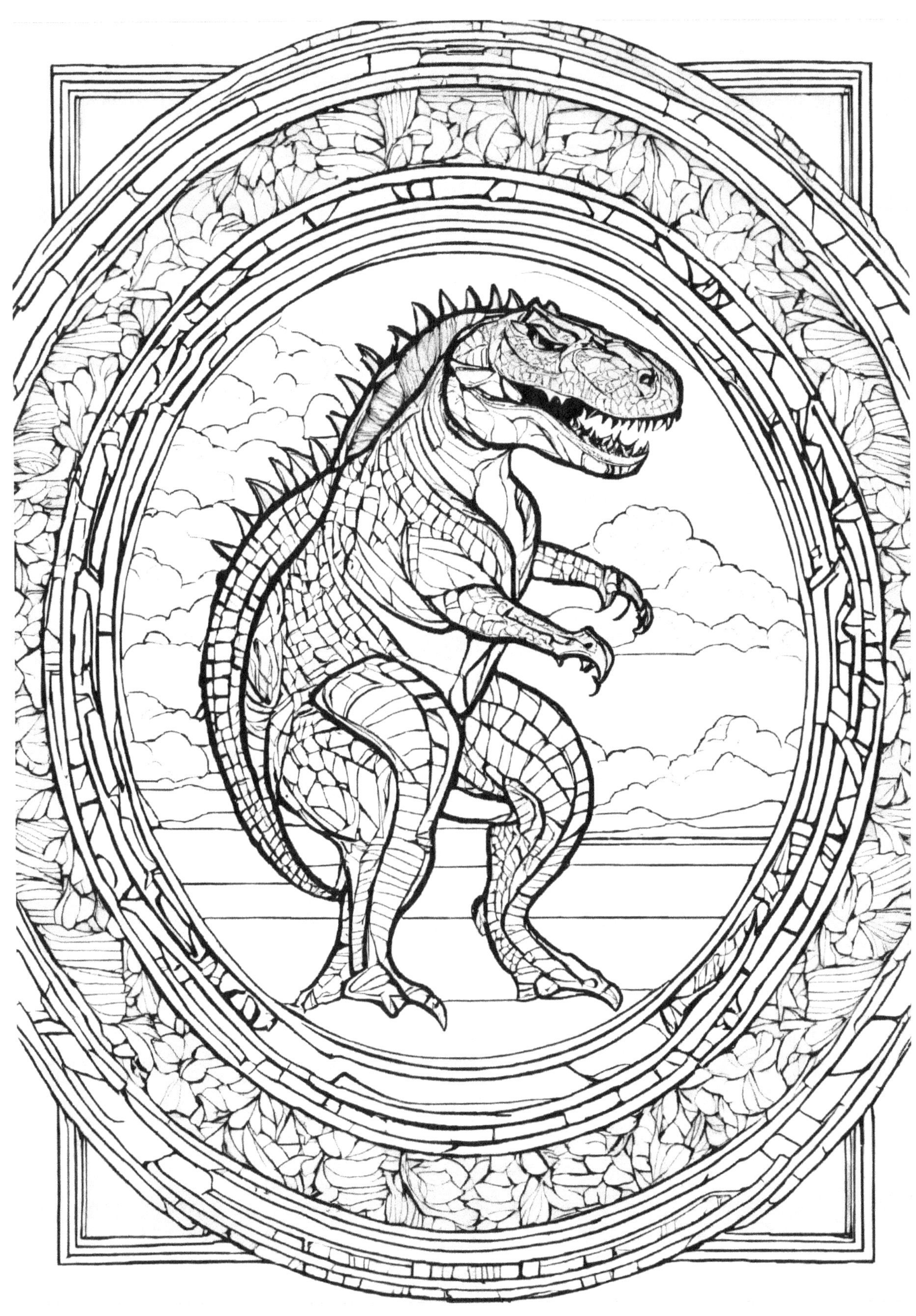

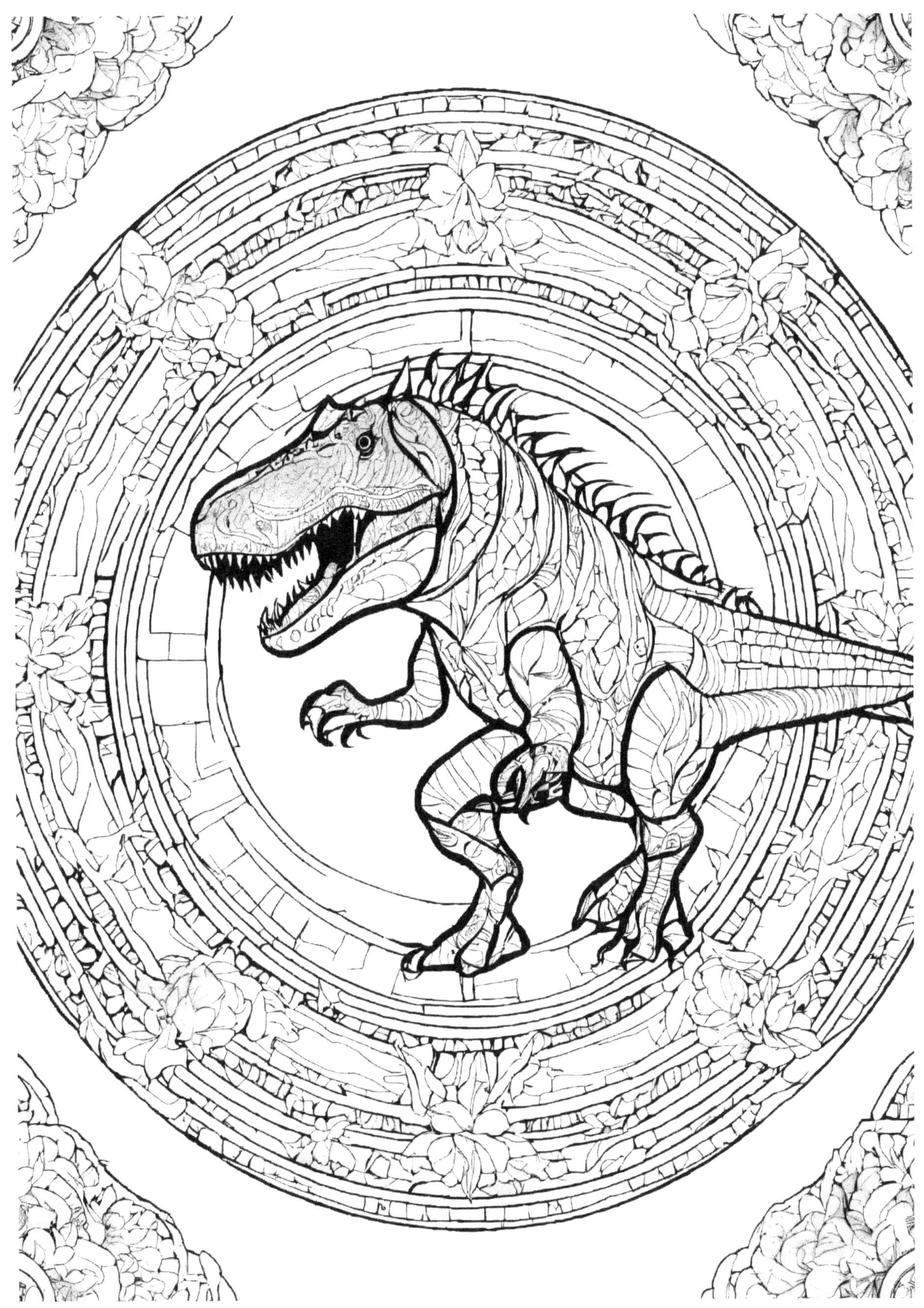

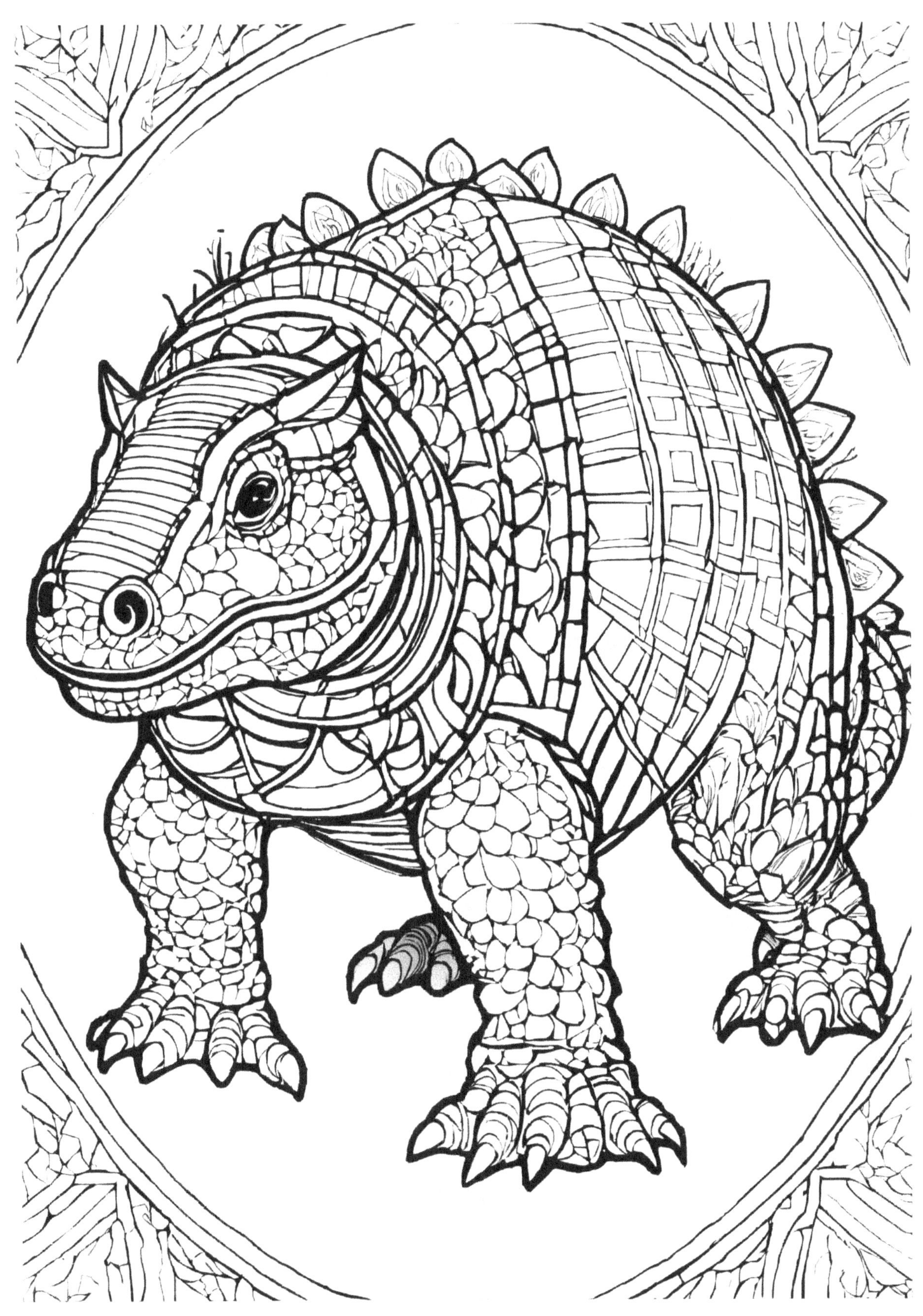

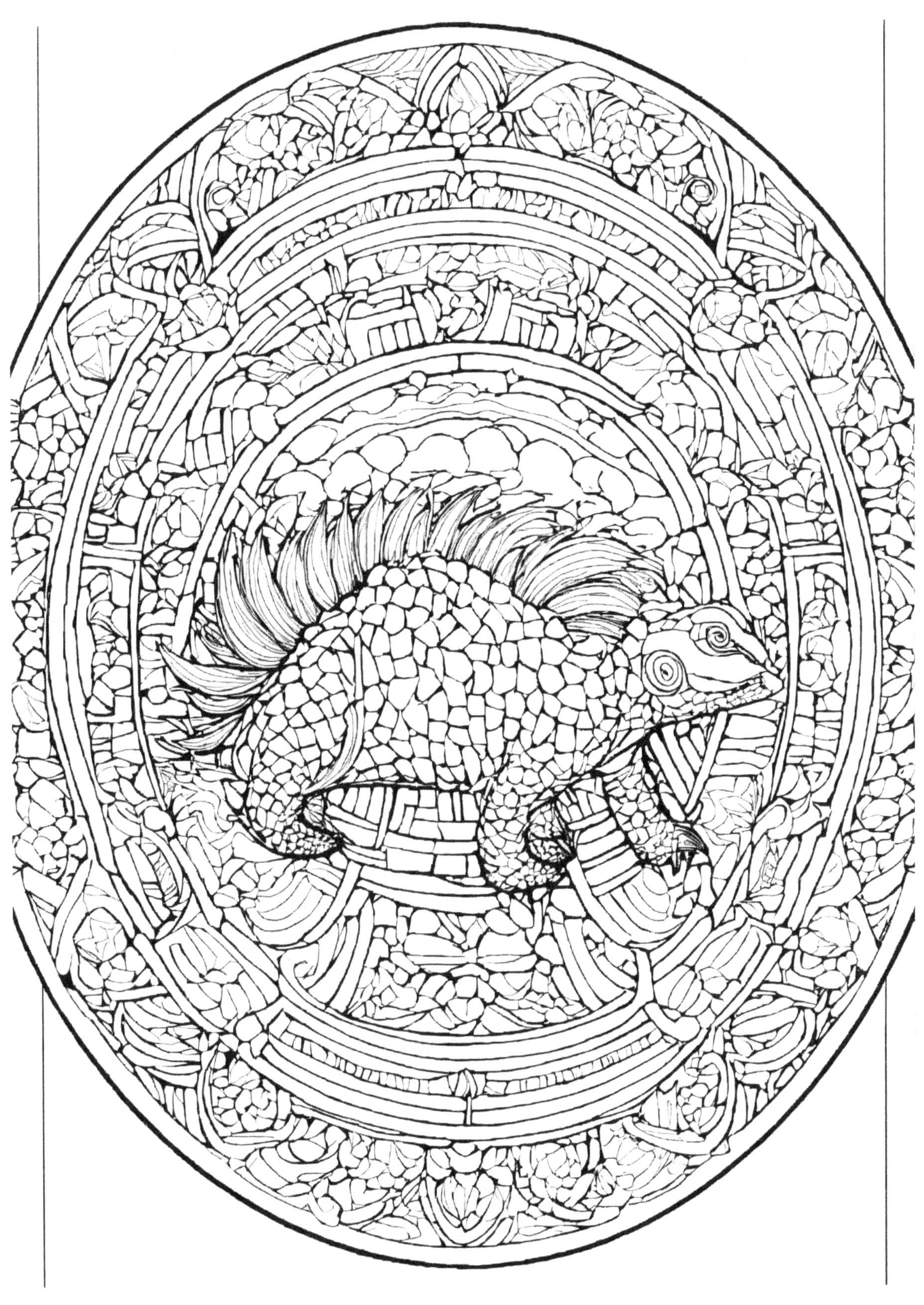

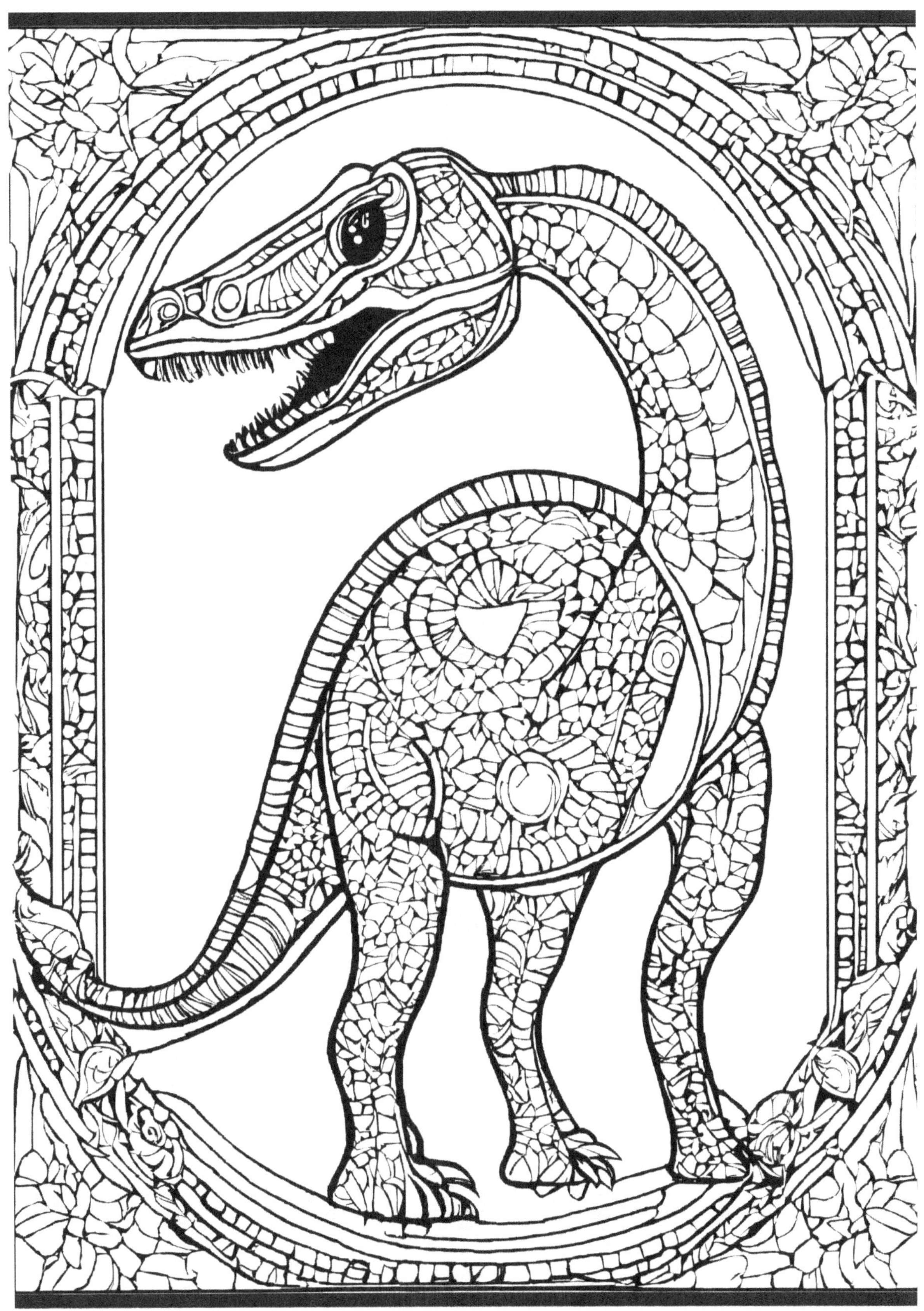

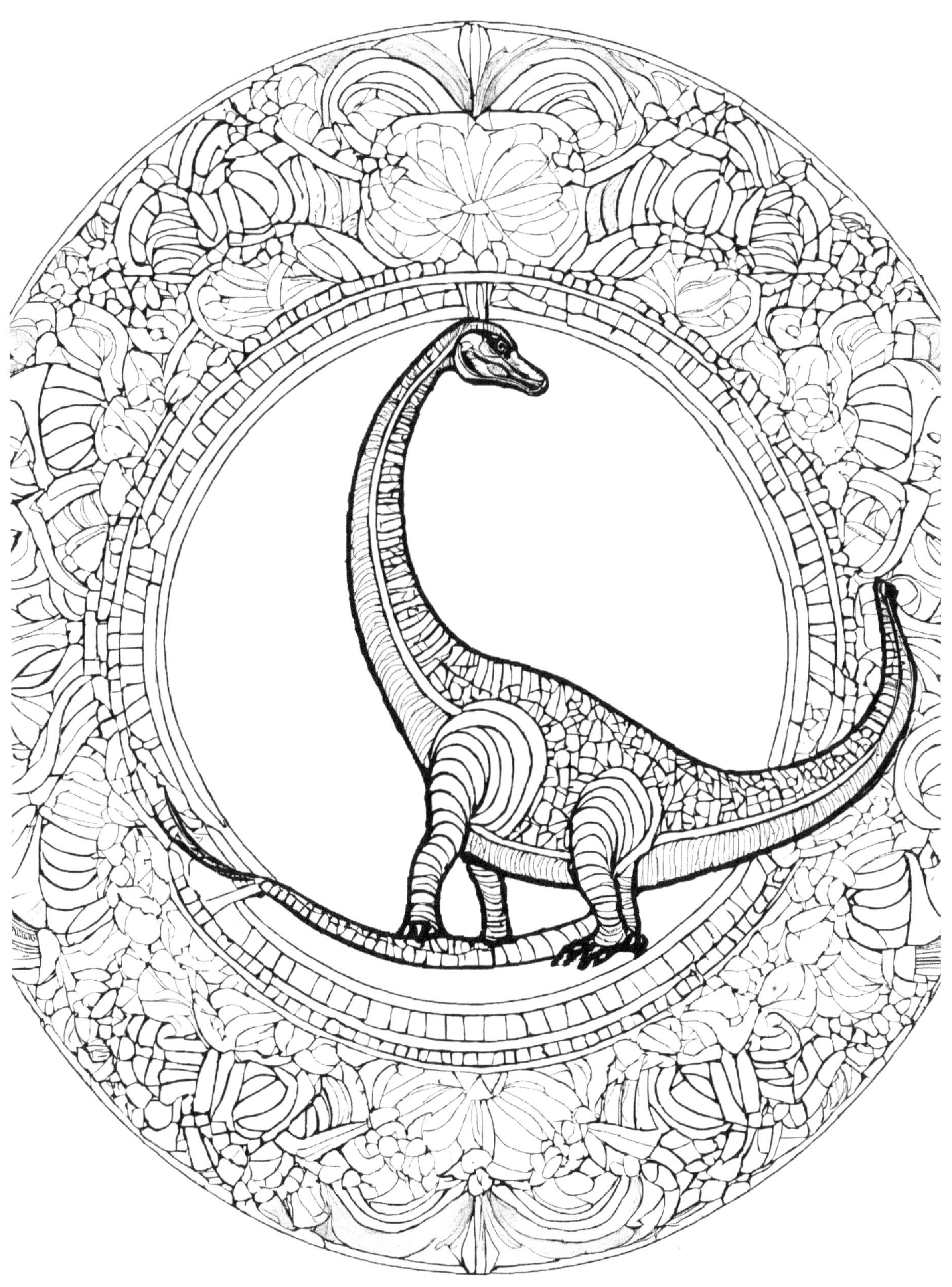

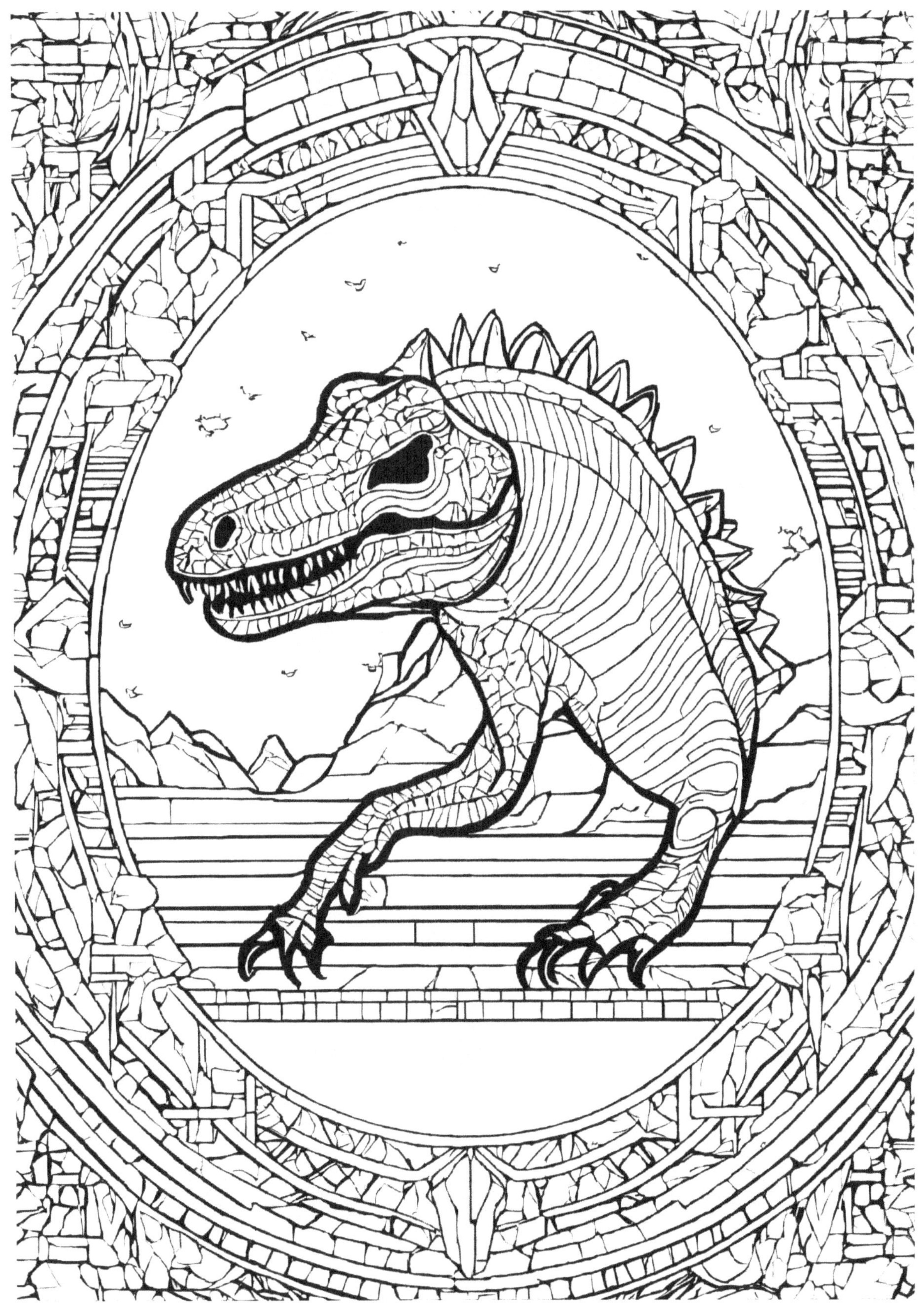

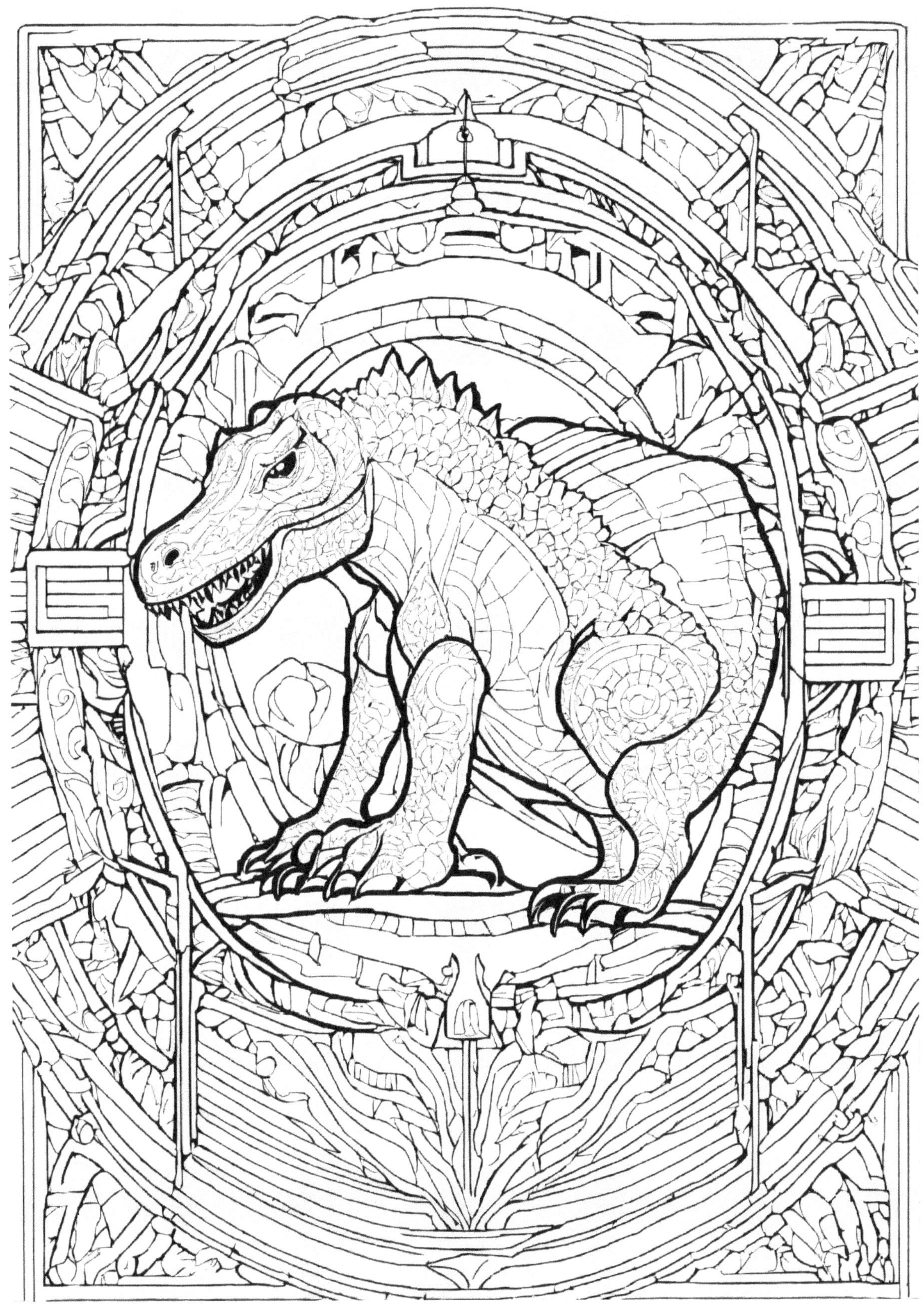

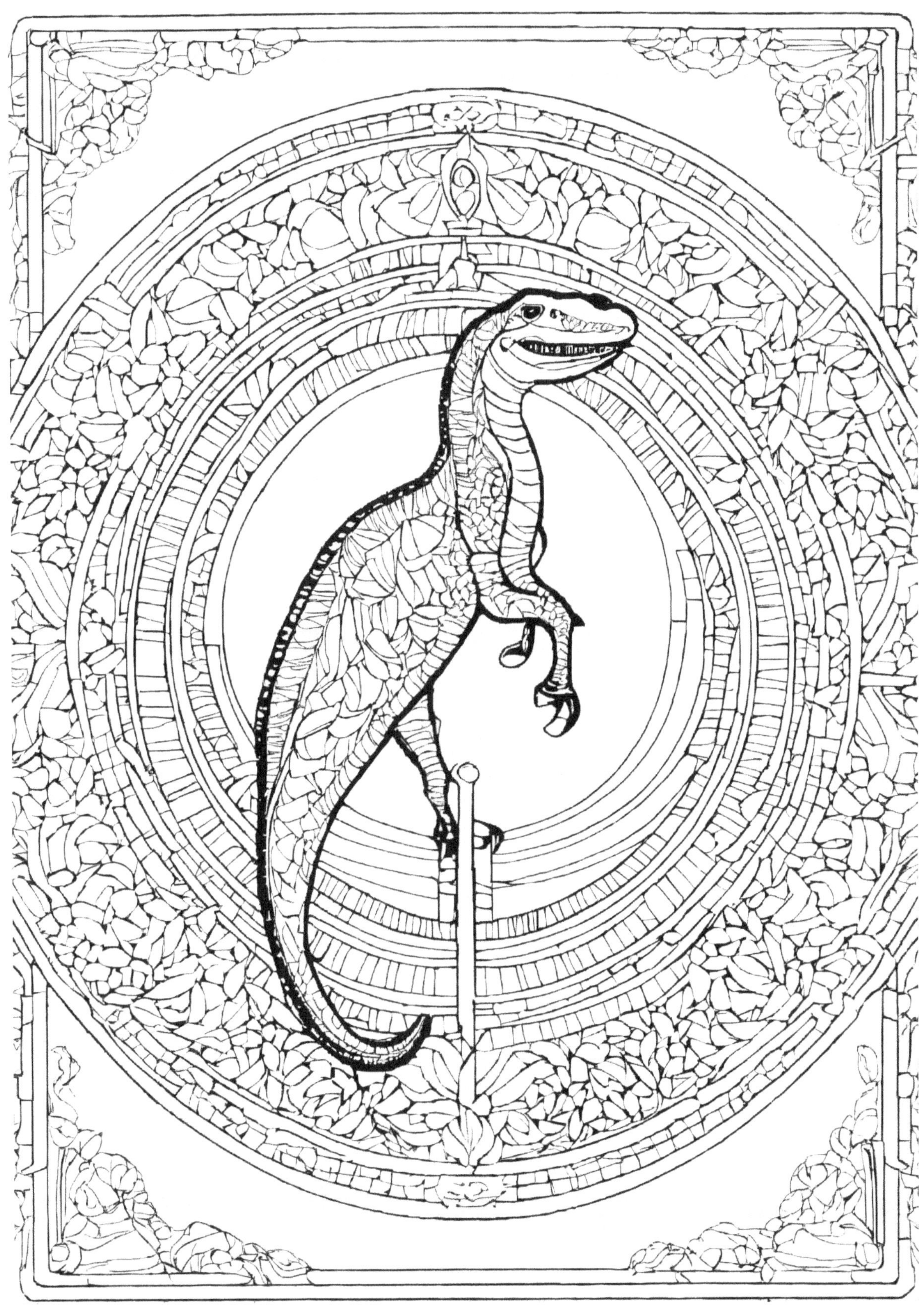

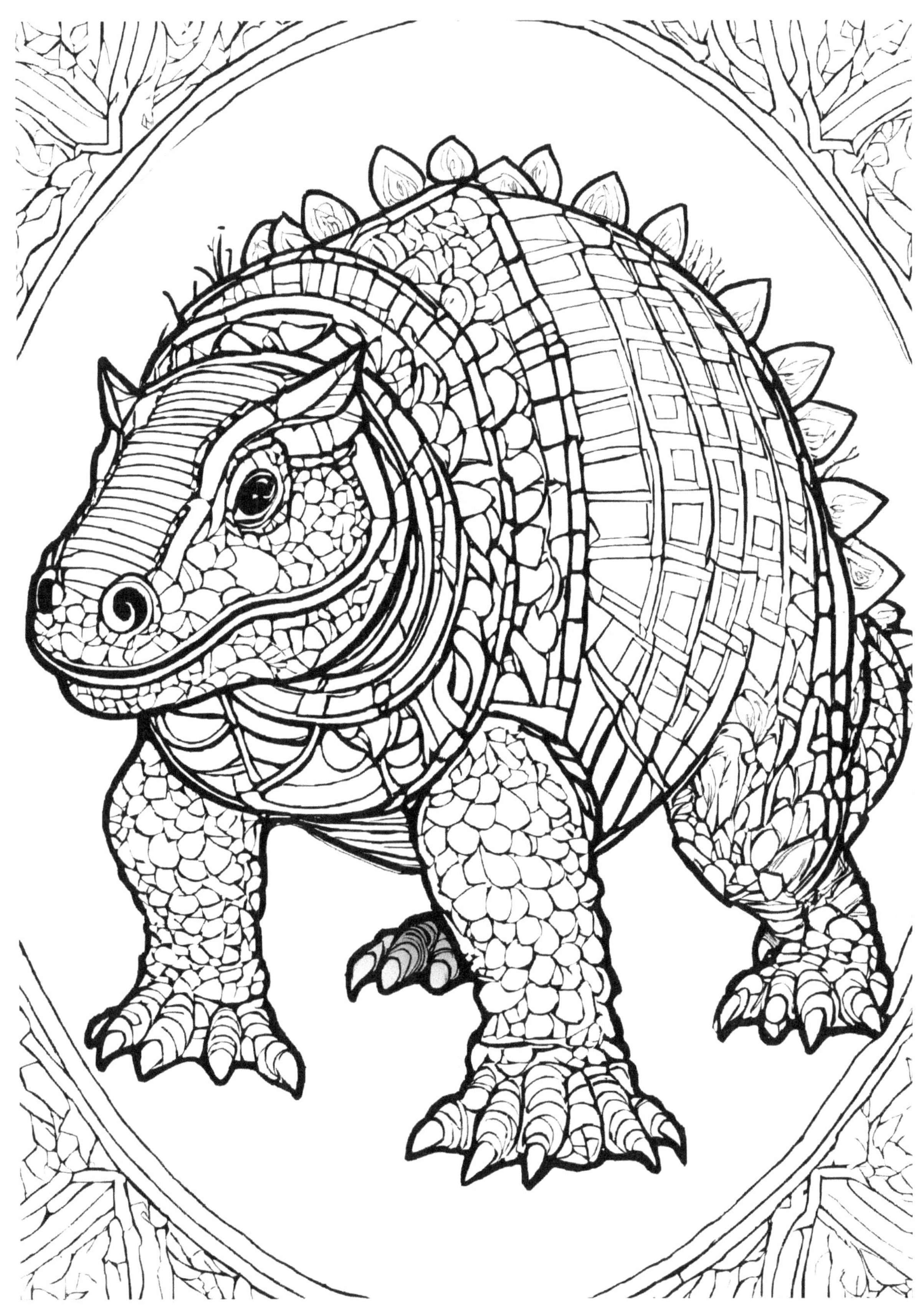

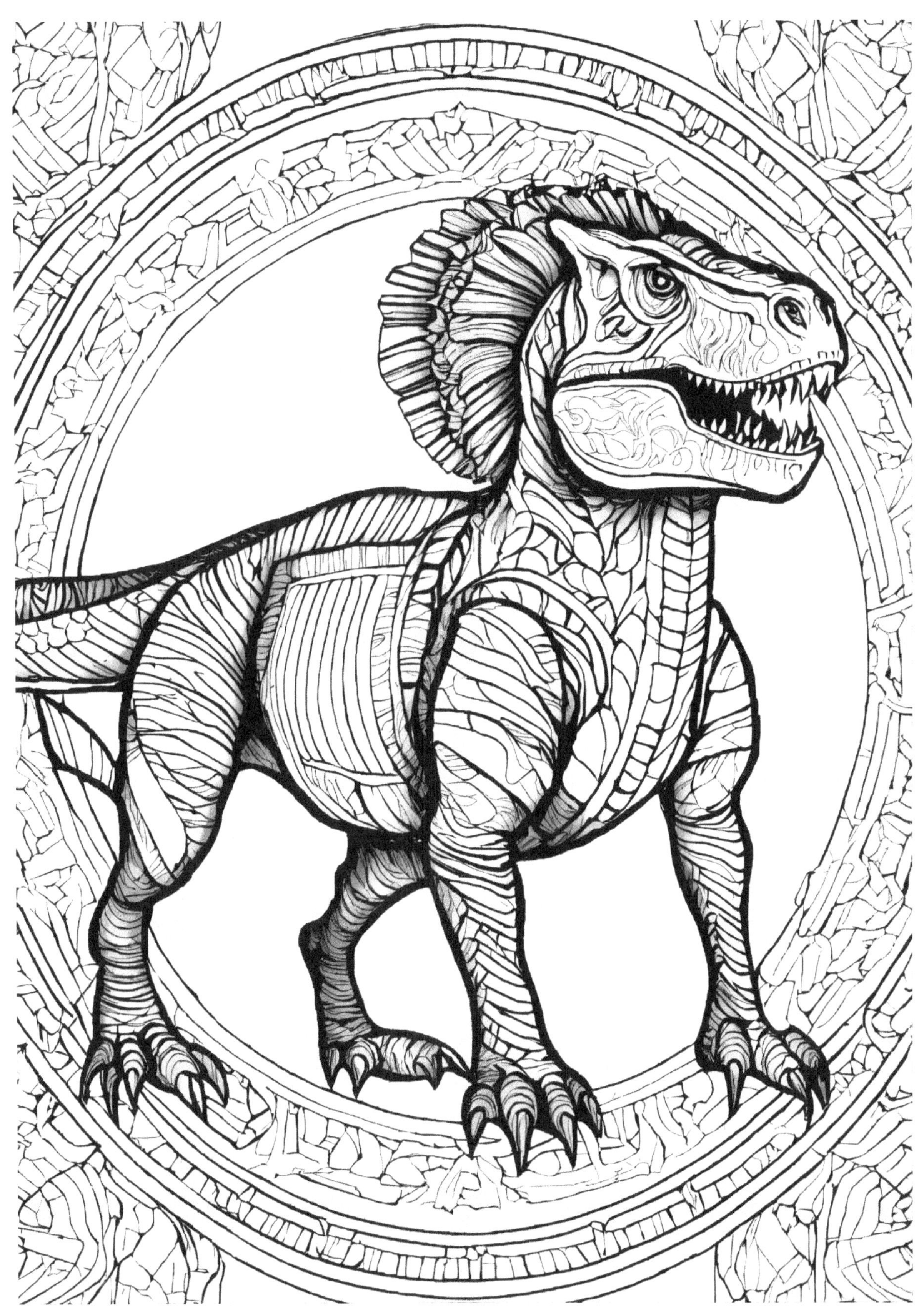

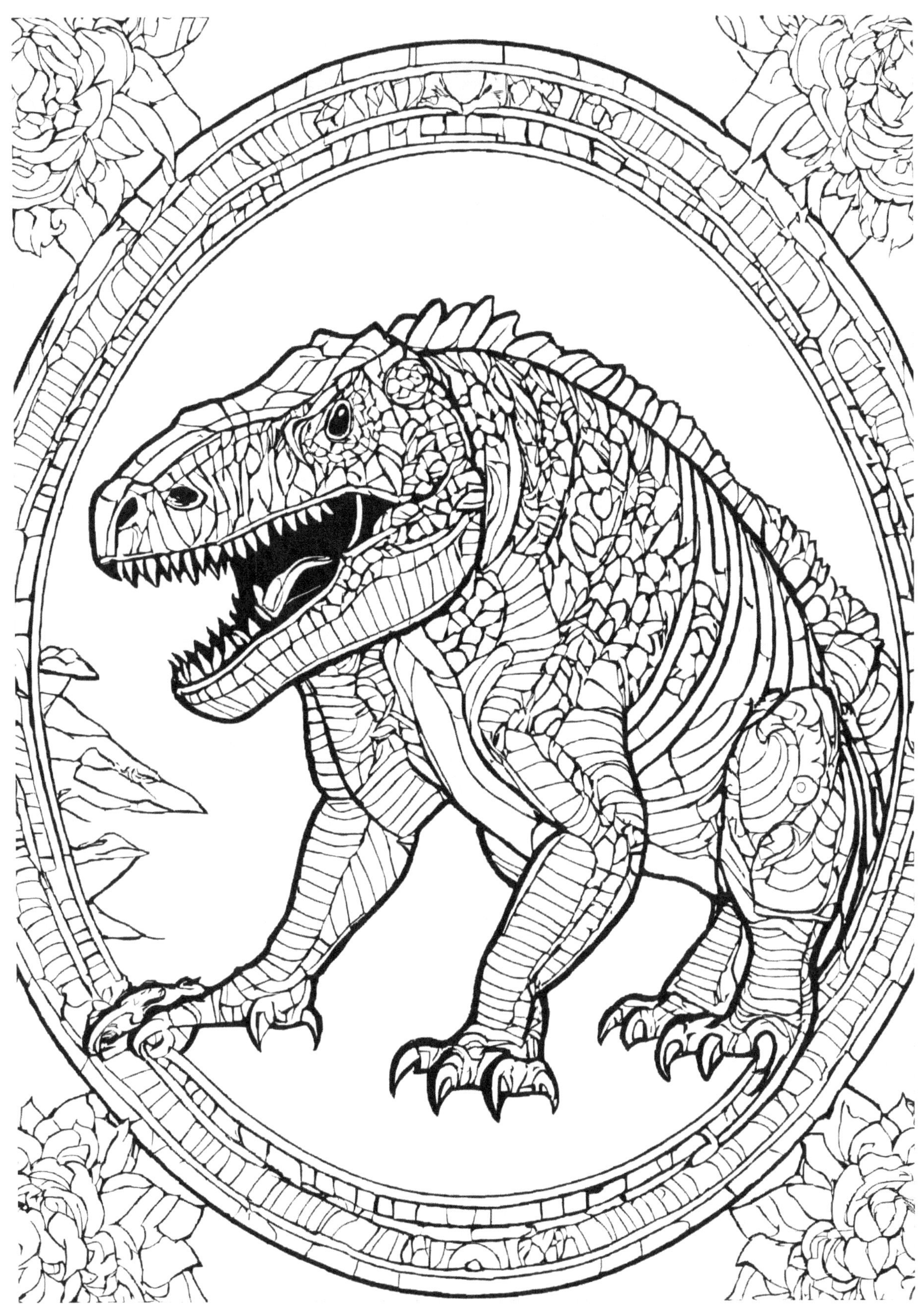

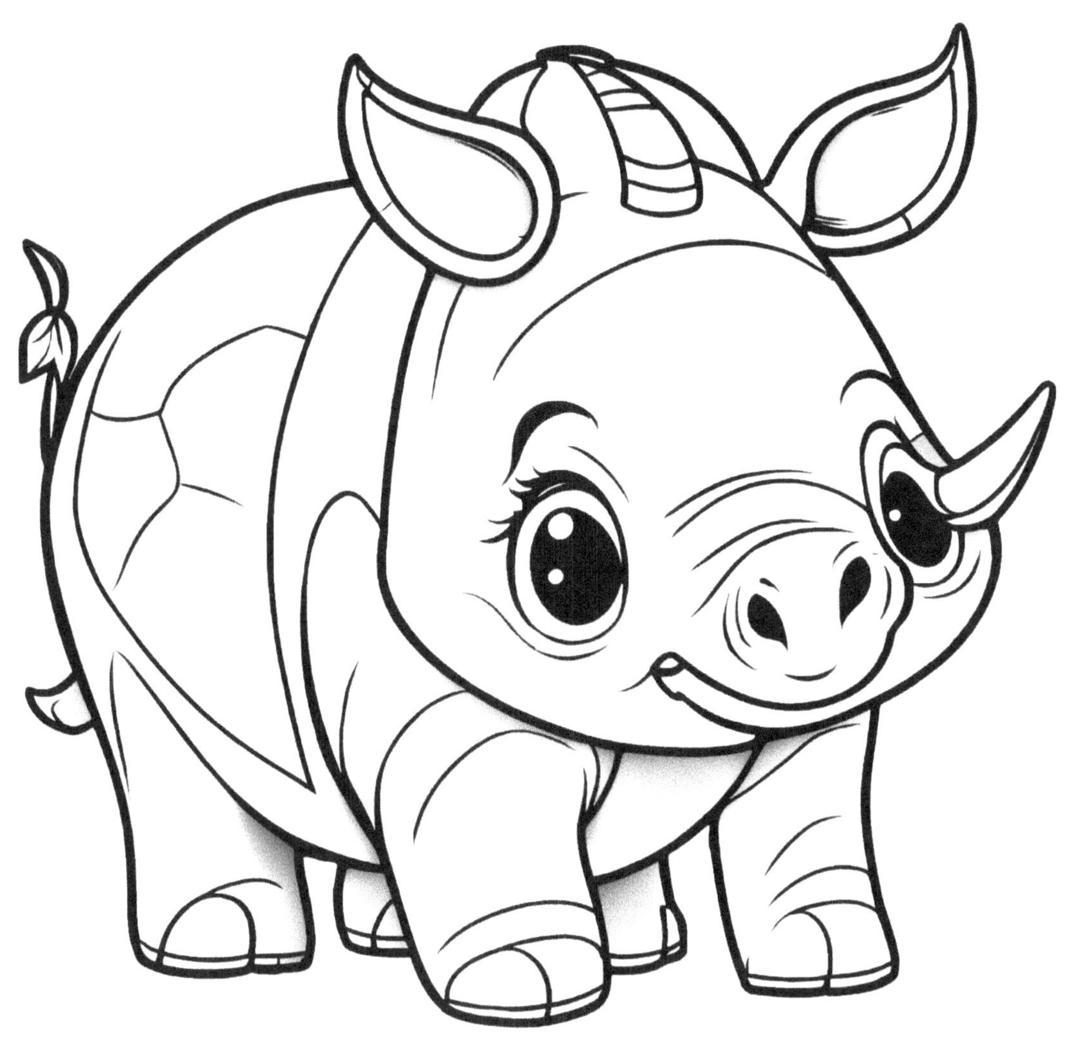

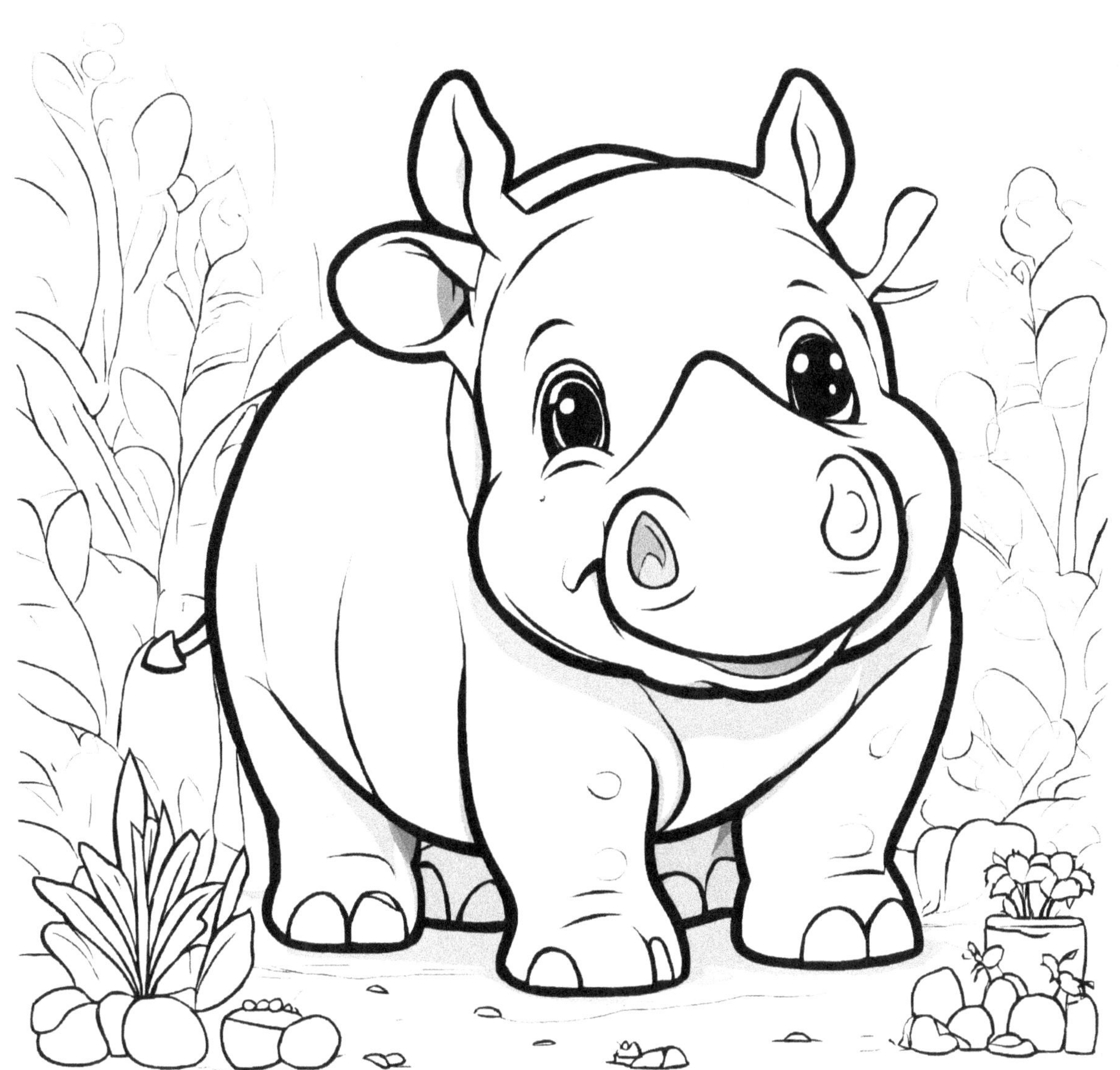

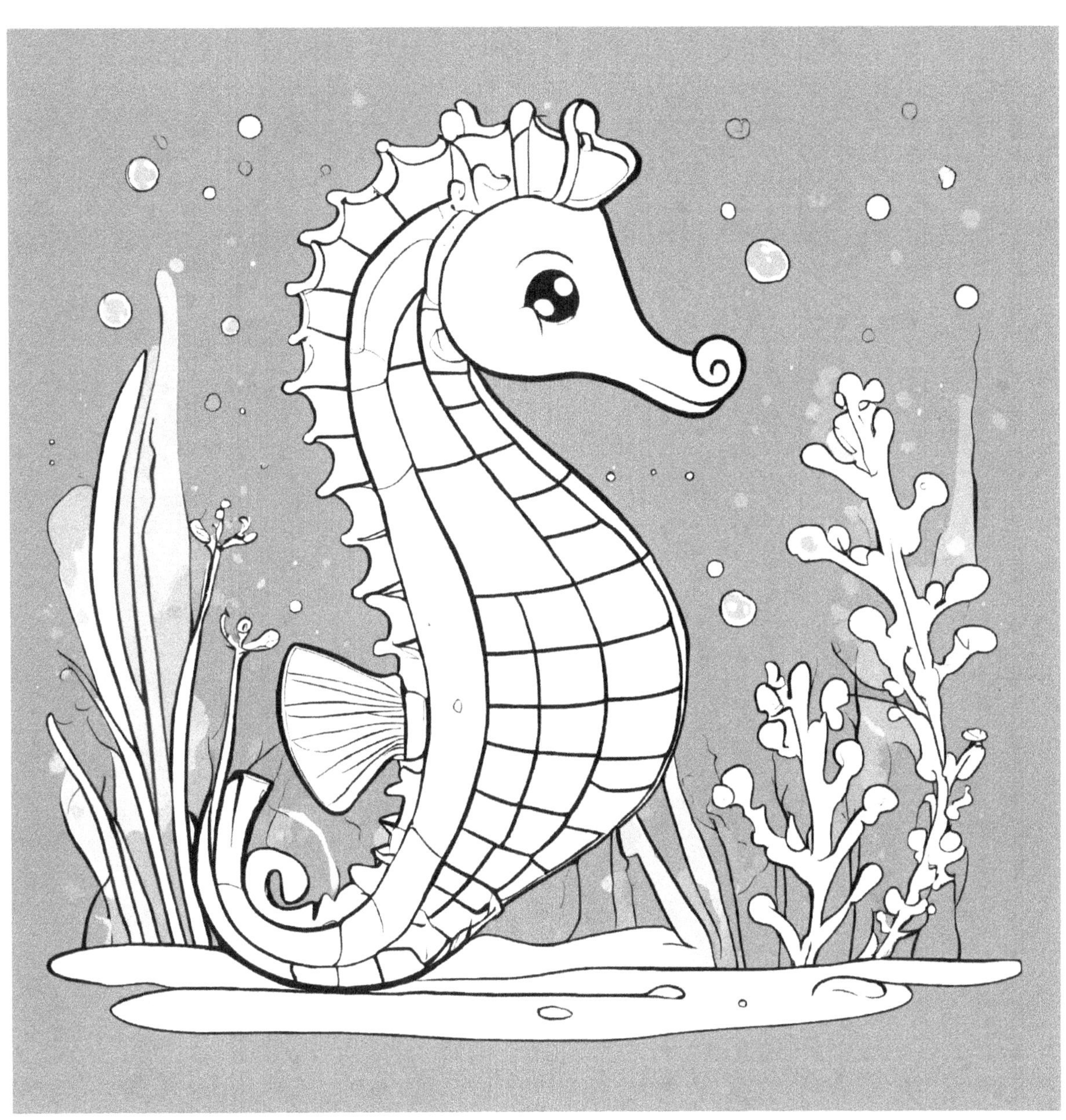

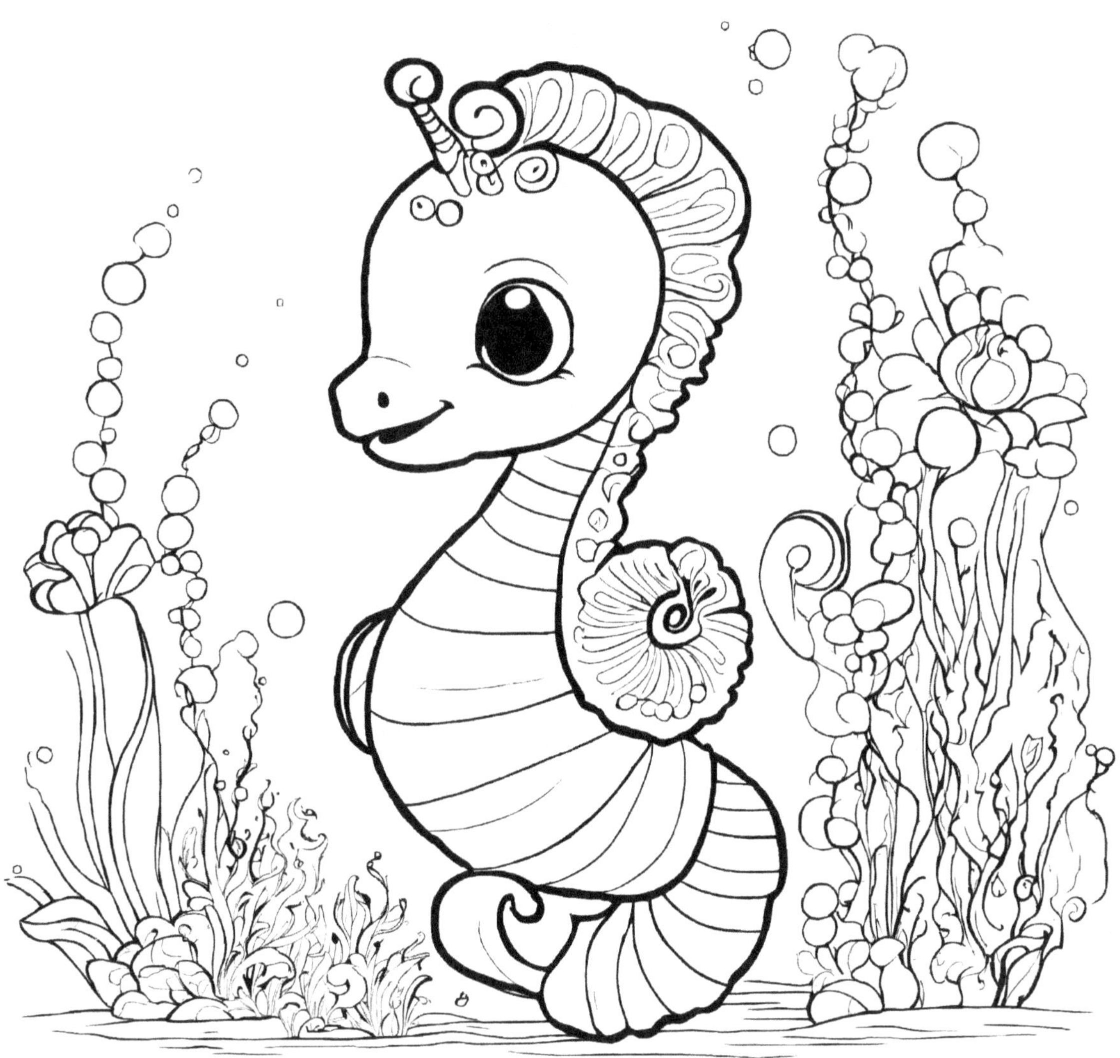

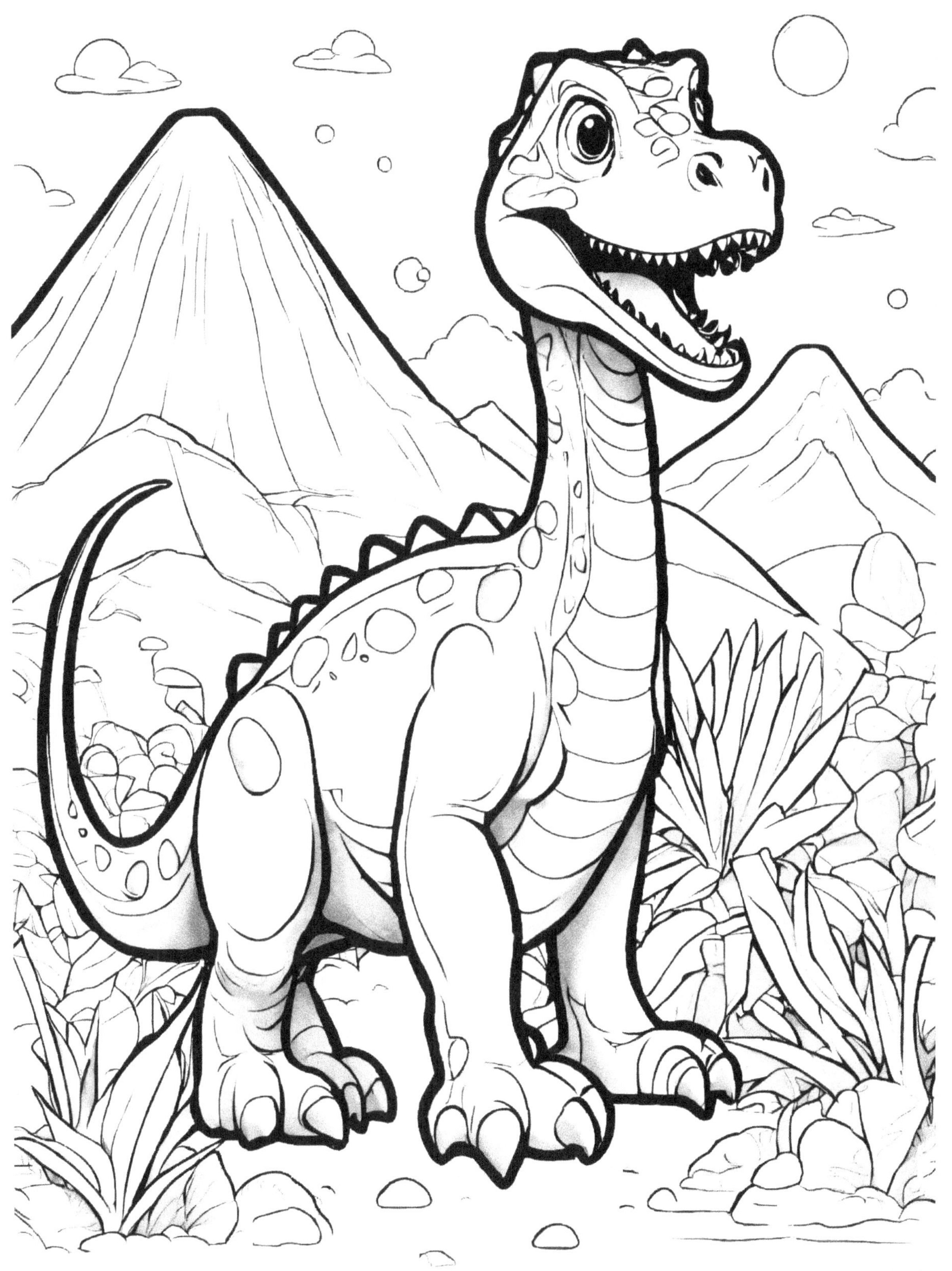